Cries of Earth and Altar

Cries of Earth and Altar

POEMS THAT COULDN'T BE HELPED

with Concluding Essay
What "Is" Is—and Isn't:
The Fragile Indicative of Poetry and Preaching

Charles L. Bartow

CASCADE *Books* • Eugene, Oregon

CRIES OF EARTH AND ALTAR
Poems That Couldn't Be Helped

Copyright © 2014 Charles L. Bartow. All rights reserved. Except for brief quotations in critical publications or reviews, no part of this book may be reproduced in any manner without prior written permission from the publisher. Write: Permissions, Wipf and Stock Publishers, 199 W. 8th Ave., Suite 3, Eugene, OR 97401.

Cascade Books
An Imprint of Wipf and Stock Publishers
199 W. 8th Ave., Suite 3
Eugene, OR 97401

www.wipfandstock.com

ISBN 13: 978-1-62564-946-1

Cataloging-in-Publication data:

Bartow, Charles L.

Cries of earth and altar : poems that couldn't be helped / Charles L. Bartow.

xvi + 124 p. ; 23 cm. —Includes bibliographical references.

ISBN 13: 978-1-62564-946-1

1. Poetry. 2. Christian Poetry, American. I. Title.

PS3553 A2 B3 2014

Manufactured in the U.S.A.

Excerpt from "An Adoration," from *The Holy Merriment* by Arnold Kenseth. Copyright © 1963 by Arnold Kenseth. Used by permission of the University of North Carolina Press. www.uncpress.unc.edu

Quotation from "Psalm 23" by Catherine Sasanov in Lynn Domina, ed., *Poets on the Psalms*. San Antonio: Trinity University Press, 2008. Used by permission of Catherine Sasanov.

In Grateful Memory of Paul E. Scherer
Preacher, Poet, Scholar, Teacher, Mentor, and Friend

Contents

Preface | xi

Introduction | xv

Advent – Epiphany   1

OUT OF WOMAN | 2
AN ADVENT INVOCATION | 3
NATIVITY'S VERDICT | 4
CHRISTMAS EVE REMEMBRANCE AND CONFESSION | 5
LEGION: THEN AND NOW | 11
A NEW YEAR'S CHRISTMAS COME | 13
EPIPHANY | 14
EPIPHANY IN DECLINE | 15

Transfiguration Sunday Meditation   17

Celebration – Psalm 19:1–6 | 19
    A HINT OF COSMIC CHEER | 21
Lamentation – Psalm 139:1–4; 11–12 | 22
    TONIGHT NO EVENING STAR | 24
Transfiguration – Psalm 50:1–6 | 25
    VENI CREATOR SPIRITUS | 27

Lent – Pentecost   29

ZACCHAEUS | 31
LAMB I AM—NOT | 32

HIS FATHER'S BUSINESS | 33
COLD CALCULATION | 38
AN AGONISTIC HYMN | 39
THE MOURNING AFTER EASTER | 45
CREATIO EX NIHILO | 46
SUPPLICATION | 47
A QUESTION OF BEATITUDE | 48

Ordinary time   49

LISTEN! | 51
THE DUCK POND | 52
TĚNEBRAE | 53
TO THE CONTRARY | 54
INTERROGATION | 55
SPRING'S GLAD LABOR | 56
BARBED TRAILS OF THOUGHT | 57
RABBIT FOOD | 58
PLANGENCY'S DRINKING SONG | 59
TORTOISE MEN | 60
AN INSOMNIAC'S QUESTION | 61
THE TRIUMPH OF *TAMIUS STRIATUS* | 62
AN AGING, PORTLY POET-PREACHER'S CONFESSION | 63
BRIEFLY STATED | 63
A TRIBUTE | 64
I DREAMT A HUMAN SKULL | 66
AFTER PRAYERS, A FACE | 67
TIME'S RECKONING | 68
AN EAST SIDE WISH | 69
IN ANTICIPATION OF DEMENTIA | 70
DELIRIUMS | 71
THE GROCER'S LARGESS | 72
ABREACTION | 73
QUESTIONS OF FAMINE | 74
AN ANTINOMIAN DAWN | 75
ECCLESIASTES REDUX | 76

CONTENTS

FALSE ALARM | 77
WHAT IS THIS YEARNING? | 78

Poems Out of Season: Back Acre Remembrances   79
(Composed in 2009)

CONCORD GRAPES | 81
VICTORY GARDEN, 1943 | 82
THE SHAMBLES COOP | 84
STRAWBERRY PATCH WORK CHRISTIANS | 86
BANISHED EDEN | 88

More Poems Out of Season: Labor Loved   93
(Composed in 2013)

OUR FAMILY FARM | 95
THE HOUSE OF MEMORY | 98
A GRUDGING RESPECT | 99
A LONG HOSPITALITY | 99
A NURTURED HOPE | 100
A BRIGHTENED LABOR | 101
A BLOSSOMED SNOW STORM | 102
FROZEN BEAUTY | 103

Concluding Essay – What "Is" Is—and Isn't:
    The Fragile Indicative of Poetry and Preaching | 105

Bibliography | 123

Preface

> O God of earth and altar,
> Bow down and hear our cry.
> —G. K. CHESTERTON, 1906

Poems, like biblical psalms, are cries of earth to the altar of the eternal. Whether praise or lamentation, they assault heaven's ear with whatever earth has on its mind and heart, and in its bowels. There is no cry of earth, doubt-filled, trust-filled, tender, glad, or furious, that is not borne on wings of prayer to heaven's high altar which, as Calvin observed, is Christ himself.[1] That altar alone can bear the weight of what dignifies and shames us: our meant and unmeant vows, our use and abuse of each other's names (and the divine name), the sometimes violent outrage of our speech and martial technology, our well-intentioned, yet often insipid, calls for peace apart from justice and in careless disregard of human enmity toward God.

Once in a televised interview, as I remember it, I heard Wynton Marsalis, that supreme poet of trumpet song, classical and jazz, speak of what music finally has to sing about. He said it sings of love and of God. Just so, like the hymnody of ancient Israel and of all hymnody since, it is instant with human aspiration and the terrible groans of our degradation. So it is with poems, whether composed by acknowledged masters or by lesser souls who must live, and die, and sing beyond their means.

I was seated at my desk in 103 Templeton Hall, Princeton Theological Seminary. The year was 2008, the year preceding my retirement. My younger colleague and friend, Michael Hegeman, stepped in. Mike, a quietly accomplished poet, musician, and composer, always, it seemed, had

---

1. Calvin, *Institutes of the Christian Religion*, 120.

PREFACE

a word to "make my day." I looked up and spoke: "Mike," I said, "I've just finished reading again Yeats', 'The Mother of God.' If in the world there is such poetic accomplishment to command 'recital and the live friction of voice and ear,'[2] why should I even try?" Mike's reply was immediate and memorable: "Because you can't help it," he said.

What follows, then, are poems that couldn't be helped. Nevertheless a number of people need to be thanked for having helped me turn into ink the blood of necessity. My brother, the Rev. Ernest Winfield Bartow, and my sister, Patricia May Romancheck gave me permission to mention them by name in *Back Acre Remembrances*. My secretary, Marija S. DiViaio, with great diligence, competence, and care took my hand-scribbled compositions and turned them into typed and digitized texts ready for submission to the publisher. The congregants of the Presbyterian Church of Deep Run (Bedminster, Bucks County, Pennsylvania), back in the 1970's encouraged my attempts now and then to proclaim the gospel through the performance of scripture, poetry, and music. More recently, under the pastoral leadership of the Rev. Ms. Elizabeth Lymon and Associate Pastor, the Rev. Ms. Sharyl Marshall, the "Deep Runners," as they are affectionately known, honored me with the designation, Pastor Emeritus. I could not possibly be more grateful for that kindness. I need to thank my colleague in preaching, theology, and the arts, Clayton J. Schmit for encouraging me to publish my first book of poetry, *Dust and Prayers: Poems* (Cascade Books, 2009). Great thanks is due as well to Paul Undreiner who set five of the poems in *Dust and Prayers* to music and to Benjamin T. Berman, tenor who sang the premier performances so beautifully. As always, my wife of nearly fifty years, Ruth Paula Goetschius Bartow, has honored me with her love, companionship, wise counsel, and prayers. She deserves and has my deepest thanksgiving for all she means to me.

Not least, the church catholic, with its heritage of doctrine and worship, has provided me with inspiration and a framework for ordering the poems offered in this volume. The arrangement rather loosely follows the themes, though only rarely the suggested lessons, of the Christian liturgical calendar. Indeed not every poem is provoked by a biblical text, and many of the poems were composed out of season, so to speak, and later inserted into what seemed an appropriate space in the liturgical calendar. Therefore, I have provided the actual date of completion of each poem following the poetic text. The sections of poetry clearly labeled "out of season," that is,

2. Steiner, *Language and Silence*, 257

PREFACE

Back Acre Remembrances and *Labor Loved*, are, if it may be allowed, an autobiographical coda to the text of poems as a whole. In season or out, it is hoped that these poems may find some resonance in the lived experience of our present moment.

Charles L. Bartow
Ramsey, NJ
16 October 2013

Introduction

Word, Sacrament, and the Christian Year

The heartbeat of worship is Word and Sacrament. And the rhythm of the Christian Year (and of the liturgical calendar), however understood in particular Christian communions, is the rhythm of nature and of human nature reset according to the heartbeat of worship. Therefore:

CHRISTOPHANY AND EUCHARIST

Blessed are those who have not seen and yet have come to believe (John 20:29b).

> I see you with the calloused crews
> At work in fields harvesting grain,
> And with youths suckering the vines
> On vineyard hills refreshed with rain,
> And, with this bread and wine, receive
> The yield of labor not in vain.
> I hear the Word that breaks the loaf,
> That pours the cup, that speaks your name.

29 March, 2014

Advent – Epiphany

If thou wilt foyle thy foes with joy,
Then flit not from this heavenly boy.[1]

ROBERT SOUTHWELL
16ᵀᴴ CENTURY

---

1. Southwell, "New Heaven, New Warre," in Walsh, *Garlands for Christmas*, 30.

OUT OF WOMAN

"Then the man said, 'This at last is bone of my bones and flesh of my flesh; this one shall be called Woman, for out of Man this one was taken'"
(Genesis 2:23)

"Blessed are you among women, and blessed is the fruit of your womb" (Luke 1:42)

". . . conceived by the Holy Ghost, born of the Virgin Mary . . ."
(The Apostles' Creed)

The angel Gabriel, God-sent, we're told,
Arrived at the virginal door, entered
With a knock of promise, and left Spirit,
Seminal life, to nurture infant flesh
In maiden bliss, vibrant, hospitable.
"Let it be with me," she'd said, no reserve,
"According to your word." And that was that.
The Spirit-flesh grew, announced readiness
To be born, to suffer. Her suffering,
Love's labor, brought to rude nativity
The angel-promised Child, the Son of God
And blessed Mary's boy, her very own,
Bone of her bone, flesh of her flesh alone.
Out of Woman, the "Man of sorrows" grown.

16 September 2010

AN ADVENT INVOCATION

To Christ Jesus: God's Son, Our Savior

After your first visit we split in two
Both history and our own thoughts of you,
Seeming as you were truly heaven sent
Yet surely of the earth, earthy as bent
Laborers tilling soil, or laying stone,
Or stitching thread, or lives, or time to own
Some happiness in work, some scent of love,
Some gladness in the thought, that far above
The cruel industry of grinding fate,
A kinder providence had set a date
To work its wonders: out of human strain
And stress, divine anguish, the awful pain
Your visit led to (for yourself the most),
Some comfort, justice, joy. Come Holy Ghost!

13 SEPTEMBER, 2010

NATIVITY'S VERDICT

(Matthew 2:1–8; Luke 2:8–20)

A stable-cry shatters the onyx sky
Into myriad crystals ringing joy,
Singing hope through the Herodian dark.
Coarse men, swarthy, stinking of sheep and sweat,
Start at the sound and sight, get word of peace,
Run as instructed to the rude manger
Where angel-dreams cradle heaven's tidings
To safety from tyranny's child-vexed weal.
The shepherds tell it all. All are amazed
At what they tell, not least we who ponder
With mother Mary the disquieting
Events of this night—the shattering cry,
The ringing, singing, news-filled onyx sky:
No peace for those with whom God is not pleased?

28 JULY, 2009

CHRISTMAS EVE REMEMBRANCE AND CONFESSION

(Matthew 2:16–18)

"What stables here
Is time for us to give our sin
The shape of kneeling." Arnold Kenseth, *An Adoration*

Darrell's apartment on Houston Street
Was dark as the night.
Even the front stairs and doorway
Were shrouded in December bleakness.
There was a dusting of dry snow
On the sidewalk; but you would have been
Hard pressed to recognize it
For what it was, for it was mixed
With fine, black soot, and the dull light
From the street lamp a half block away
Did nothing to illumine it.
"What a god-forsaken place,"
I thought, as I got out of the car
With the rest of Darrell's friends.
"Who on earth would want to live here?
How could a person survive?"

That survival would not have been
Easy, was clear enough
Not only from the look of the place
But also from the feel of it.
It was bitter cold.
One whiff of the air
And my nostrils stuck shut.

One sucked-in breath and my skeleton
Quivered in its sack
Of flesh and muscle.
Tonight, at least,
Houston Street was cruel.
The elements conspired to prove that.
There was no doubting
Their inhospitable counsel:
"Find a spot inside and warmer;
Leave us alone." I hurried
To oblige. Far be it from me
To overstay my welcome
Anywhere, and here especially.
Behind the drawn shades of Darrell's place
Lights waited, and laughter, food, drinks, heat.
You could hardly keep me from it.

My friends hurried too, anxious to get in,
But not too anxious to talk.
We were always talking. "Weird,
Isn't it!" Doug exclaimed.
"Oh, I don't know," said Eileen;
"Not if you know Darrell.
I think the place suits him. There he is
Hunkered down in a laughing spot
Up above this soot and wintry
Bleakness, making Christmas happen.
Just like him, I'd say.
Just what you might expect."

Just what you might *not* expect
Passed us by at that moment:
Three against the cold, two talking,
One silent—mouth open, red, raw,

Eyes fixed, arms, legs exposed, stiff,
Struck out against the night
In mute protest—as grotesque
A sight as you could come up against
Ever. "Did you see that?"
Each of us said in turn,
Passing round our astonishment.
Of course each of us saw it.
But once that fact was assured
By our circling question,
No further word was spoken.
Call it shock, disbelief, call it
What you will, there was no more said,
And nothing done. Doug reached the door,
Rang for Darrell, and in we went
Out of the cold, and away from what
Just now had frozen our thoughts
And stifled our conversation.
We joined the party.

There was plenty to eat, plenty
To drink. Some of the conversation
Wasn't fit for Christmas.
You'll want to know about that,
I'm sure. But I'll not tell you. No,
Don't ask me. Later maybe
I'll fill you in, when we've plenty of time
And little or nothing to gain
Or lose from a wasted moment.
Right now, though, there's a matter
Needs going into, and I want your help.
It's near Christmas again, after all,
The very eve of it, and I don't know
If I can handle that without your help.

We've kept silent too long, all of us.
We couldn't face what we left
Out on that street, you see,
When we went in to Darrell's party.
We couldn't bear the memory of it
Even in the second after we saw it.
For long, long years we've been shut up.
But now the things there, right there,
Between me and Christmas,
Between all of us and Christmas.
It's between us and Bethlehem,
And the manger, and the baby
Jesus, and the dark, brutal moment
When King Herod said: "Kill
The children! Kill the children!"

I believe they must have killed
The child. The mother and daughter did it,
I suppose, or the aunt and cousin,
Or friends picked up from somewhere.
I don't know. The three against the cold,
That's who they were: two grown women,
One older, one younger, and one baby,
Almost naked, bared to the freezing winds
That had caught my breath and my friends',
And sent us hurried for Darrell's door.
You don't believe it, or can't, or won't.
That doesn't matter. I believe
They must have killed the child.
They looked poor. They looked desperate.
They looked worried and alone;
And they talked excitedly,
But not out loud. So we couldn't
Tell what was said or meant.

We could only tell what must have been
Their purpose. Stop them? Help them?
We couldn't help ourselves.

Tell me, do you think *he* knows,
The one who lived when the babies died,
When King Herod said: "Kill the children"?
Do you think he knows
About Houston Street,
Sees or cries, or cares?
I told you I needed your help
To face this Christmas, and I need his.
I could face it, I really believe
I could, if I knew he cared,
Could see that baby,
Those desperate women,
And hear us all shut up.

Darrell's apartment on Houston Street
Was left the way we found it, shades drawn
To hold in the light from any escape
Into New York's bleak midwinter. "It's weird,"
Doug said, "I still say this place is weird."
Eileen, for her part, persisted
In disagreement, replying
Tersely, "Well, I say it isn't."
We got into our car and headed
Home. I can tell you this,
As I think back on it,
That night, its partying and all
Its horrors. I can tell you
That there is more unfit for Christmas
Than conversation at Christmas parties.
Whole lives are unfit for it. Whole worlds

Are shrouded in December bleakness.
Our lives and our *worlds* were—and *are*—
That's for sure, just as Herod's world
Was. Don't you think? Yet maybe
That's why Christmas is so badly needed.
Maybe that's why all of us keep on
Looking for the Christmas baby,
And keep on waiting, waiting,
Waiting for the coming Christ.

14 January, 2012
From reflections dating to Christmastide, 1963

Note: I call this non-metrical, non-rhymed poem a fictionalized anecdote. The "lived moment" to which the poem bears witness was for me actual as I've spoken of it. Place names and persons' names have been changed to maintain the anonymity of those who lived the moment with me but whose recollections of it, and reflections upon it—if any—may differ from mine. "Bleak midwinter" is taken from Christina Rossetti's rightly admired poem, which begins "In the bleak midwinter, Frosty wind made moan" (c. 1872).

LEGION: THEN AND NOW

(Mark 5:1–13)

(A Christmastide Remembrance of the Deranged, and the Deceased of Newtown, Connecticut and Sites of Similar Atrocity)

The demon possessed
    In ancient times
Lived among the tombs,
    Wounding themselves
With stones—and howling.
    Shackles and chains
Could not subdue them.

The demons themselves,
    Fearing divine
    Emancipation,
    Sought release from
Torment in torment
    Of hapless lives
Rushed toward sudden death.

Rushed toward sudden death,
    Hapless lives now,
No longer pursued
    By demons, die
From possessive states
    Syndrome, mere lack
Of *self*-possession.

Then, in ancient times,
    The demon, named,
Was "legion," power,
    Alien, armed,
Holding consciousness
    In thrall. Today
Demons have no name.

But armed to the teeth
    Alien force
Still holds in thrall
    The consciousness
Of children, women—
    Men pressed into
Its cruel service.

And once the hapless
    Die, the nameless
Legions turn upon
    Their hosts, wounding
Them mortally. Spare
    The shackles and
The chains, the howling.

Dead within their tombs,
    Untormented
Emancipated
    Unself-possessed
Still, yet demon-free,
    The once possessed
Live in memory.

26 December, 2012

A NEW YEAR'S CHRISTMAS COME

So Christmas once more ends inebriate,
Its angel voices silenced by the howl
Of teary, bleary hymns to "Auld Lang Syne,"
And tipsy toasts, a slurred, "Happy New Year!"
Gay revelers carouse throughout the night
That, starless, darkens hope of "peace on earth"
And makes of heedless, happy voices strong
A coarse-tongued dirge, all unaware, lament
As deep, as long, as insensate as death.
Yet still what's proffered here, despite the din,
The New Year's gaud, earth's strife, is peace with God,
A Christmas come and yet to come again.

14 OCTOBER, 2010

EPIPHANY

At Bethlehem – The House of Bread

The ancient cosmologists read heaven
In a star—perhaps a supernova—
Heading east to west, marking heaven's way
Down into the straw and stench, the hidden
Homelessness that keeps the tyrant's conscience
Salved even as he eats the children's bread
And kicks the children's tattered, patched behinds,
While they, heedless of consequence, go on
Busting each other's chops for scattered crumbs
Not yet ground beneath the offending boot.
Is this the last, best hope of humankind,
To come here, to stop here where the star stopped,
To bow here where wise men bowed, where heaven
Bowed to show its hungry, newborn child's smile?
Will the tyrant at last come here to bow
To drink heaven's mirth from a common cup,
To eat, from a shared loaf, bread for the world?

4 OCTOBER, 2010

EPIPHANY IN DECLINE

(Sunday Morning, 8:45am)

Fall comes on now with all its promised bite,
Dawn's frost, evening's dank breath, noon's failing warmth.
Spirit's ample flesh thins soon to feel cold
Winter's burning blast of white-out weather.
The blinding clarity of freezing air
Alerts the mind to what's in store for it:
Sluggishness, some last thoughts icing over,
Summer unremembered, spring longer gone,
The past a grave for every once bright hope,
The heavy earth falling. Yet there's a sense
Of life not only behind and before
This autumn onset of the end of things,
But here, now, in the thick of dying days.
Hear choirs singing, preachers bravely preaching
That Living Word, the way, the truth, the life
For seasons coming on, forgotten, all!

18 SEPTEMBER, 2011

Transfiguration Sunday Meditation

❖ ❖ ❖

O Father, with th' eternal Son,
And Holy Spirit, ever One,
Vouchsafe to bring us by Thy grace
To see Thy glory face to face.[2]

LATIN, 15TH CENTURY
TRANS. JOHN MASON NEALE, 1854

---

2. See Jones, *The Hymnbook*, hymn 182.

Celebration

Psalm 19:1-6

The heavens are telling the glory
of God;
and the firmament proclaims
his handiwork.
Day to day pours forth speech,
and night to night declares
knowledge.
There is no speech, nor are there
words;
their voice is not heard;
Yet their voice goes out through
all the earth,
and their words to the end of
the world.

In the heavens [God] has set a tent
for the sun,
Which comes out like a
bridegroom from his
wedding canopy,
and like a strong man runs its
course with joy.
Its rising is from the end of the
heavens,
and its circuit to the end of
them;
and nothing is hid from its heat.

Comment:

It is poetry, and the Bible is full of it, both testaments, and you cannot turn it into prose. It is not a mere conjury, what the biblical poet hears and sees. It is, instead, an unimaginable immensity and beauty and promise impressed upon a divinatory imagination. Therefore, even in the winters of our discontent (to adapt a phrase from Shakespeare), we are sent to search for words to attest it: God's cheering us despite the fact that, at times, "Full desertness / In souls as countries, lieth silent-bare / Under the blanching, vertical eye-glare / Of the absolute Heavens."[3]

---

3. Elizabeth Barrett Browning, "Grief," 99.

A HINT OF COSMIC CHEER

Psalm 19:1–6

A steel gray sky at last begins to yield
To gaiety of color and of warmth,
Unusual midst January's cold
Snow-shrouded welcoming of wintry climes,
When darkest darkness overrules the day
And daylight, cut off short, shortens the time
We've got for keeping new year's promises,
Those resolutions to amend our ways
By ringing out the old and in the new,
As Tennyson allowed he heard the bells—
Lone church bells—do, so long ago, with joy:
"Ring out wild bells, to the wild sky," he sang.[4]
And yet, today, no need of bells to ring,
For suddenly the bright, wild sky itself
Rings pink and blue, a sparkling, sequined song,
A music so sublime, so clear, it turns
The eye into an ear that gladly hears,
Just in the nonce, a hint of cosmic cheer
To outlast all the darkness of the years
Now past, and wintry years still sure to come.

9 January, 2012

---

4. Alfred Lord Tennyson, "In Memoriam," 190.

Lamentation

Psalm 139:1–4; 11–12

The psalmist prays and he is not happy:

O Lord, you have searched me
and known me.
You know when I sit down and
when I rise up;
You discern my thoughts from
far away.
You search out my path and my
lying down,
and are acquainted with all
my ways.
Even before a word is on my
tongue,
O Lord, you know it
completely.

If I say, "Surely the darkness shall
cover me,
and the light around me become
night,"
even the darkness is not dark
to you;
the night is as bright as the day,
for darkness is as light to you.

Comment:

In other words, God knows us better than we know ourselves, and even what we might wish to hide from God—ever had anything to hide from God?—God inevitably finds out. That is the terror of it, and the backhanded blessing of it, that in the deepest darkness—where we hide our hates, for instance—God sees clearly as in the day, and makes of midnight memories a conscience brighter than an evening star or moon.

TONIGHT NO EVENING STAR

Psalm 139:11–12

Tonight no evening star, no moon to pierce
The steep descent of overspreading night
Or keep night's near and haunting death-owl still,
Or quiet thoughts of conscience stirred to life
From out of the darkened past, thoughts, memory,
Unbridled, brings to present consciousness:
The cruelty of subtly crafted slights,
The smiles, oft' smiled, to hide the heart's cold sneer,
Mean jokes, well told, at some poor soul's expense
For laughter from the sycophantic crowd—
Stern thoughts that drive the conscience-stricken self
At last to cringe at what it's done and said.
Disquieting the death-hoots of the owl
That haunt the starless, moonless night's descent,
Yet blessed still the dark that brings to light
What memory must cause the self to see
Since, darkened, it's not seen itself aright.

23 FEBRUARY, 2012

Transfiguration

Psalm 50:1–6

Psalm 50:1–6 is the psalm appointed for Transfiguration Sunday.

The mighty one, God the Lord,
speaks and summons the earth
from the rising of the sun to its
setting.
Out of Zion, the perfection of beauty,
God shines forth.
Our God comes and does not keep
silence,
before him is a devouring fire,
and a mighty tempest all around
him.
He calls to the heavens above
and to the earth, that he may
judge his people:
"Gather to me my faithful ones,
who made a covenant with me
by sacrifice!"
The heavens declare his
righteousness,
for God himself is judge.

Comment:

The gospel reading for transfiguration Sunday is Mark 9:2–9. You know the story: the mountain, Jesus' bright white raiment, Moses and Elijah, a cowed and fearful Peter, James, and John, the bright cloud—ever seen a bright cloud?—and the voice: "This is my Son, the beloved, listen to him" (Mark 9:7)!

There is too much to the story to tell now, but this above all must be said: The transfigured, the glorified Lord, is the Christ of the cross. And he, so the creed attests, is "to come to judge the living and the dead." And through that judgment—it is the judgment of a relentless love—we are to be made fit to share in a creation transfigured into a cathedral of God's praise. Therefore, we dare to pray boldly for the coming upon us of the Holy Ghost, the Holy Creator Spirit.

VENI CREATOR SPIRITUS

"even the darkness is not dark
to you;
the night is as bright as the day,
for darkness is as light to you" (Ps. 139:12).

The darkness that has been shall yet be still
In waiting for the breaking light that will
Encompass it with brightness beautiful,
A dawn that flick'ring shadows cannot cull,
Or comprehend, or dim, diminish, flee.
The waiting darkness will its own self see,
Made bright and glorious as endless day
With lilies white and dark-stemmed roses gay,
A silent choir to waft throughout the nave
And clerestory of nature wave on wave
Of allelujahs, nature's God to praise,
While mute humanity, startled, must gaze
In awe, then cry:
    "Come, Holy Ghost, our souls inspire,
    And lighten with celestial fire!"[5]

15 JANUARY, 2011

---

5. *Veni Creator Spiritus*, Attr. Rabanus Maurus, ninth century; translated and paraphrased by John Cosin, 1627.

Lent – Pentecost

◆ ◆ ◆

Christ rises! Mercy every way
Is infinite,—and who can say?[6]

ROBERT BROWNING
19TH CENTURY

---

6. Robert Browning, "Christmas Eve and Easter Day," 335.

ZACCHAEUS

A Soliloquy On Christ's Harrowing Of Hell

(Luke 19:1–10)

A hellish life is not impossible
To grasp, not given all I'm thought to be,
Not given what I know myself of wealth
Sequestered in the service of the vast
Conspiracy of privilege that sweeps
Through strife-torn ages to secure the pow'r
Of might to make its right adored and held
Inviolate. And yet a heav'nly life
While not so readily conceivable
As hell can still be apprehended close
At hand as love that bears clear to the end
The reprobation lovelessness deserves,
So freeing self-condemning, hell-bent selves
To unsequester wealth from selfish ends.

24 FEBRUARY, 2011

LAMB I AM—NOT

*So I find it to be a law that when I want to do
what is good, evil lies close at hand (Rom. 7:21).*

I would that I were other than I am:
So prone to do what I deem worst in me,
So little given to the best I see,
So much, it seems, a headlong rushing ram,
So seldom self-effacing as the Lamb,
So bent on taking others who knows where?
So slow to follow Wisdom, and to dare
What Wisdom teaches: love to neighbors—all,
With love to self the last, least thought to call
To mind. No hint of self-sufficiency,
But thanks to God for *His* aseity.

11 JULY, 2010

HIS FATHER'S BUSINESS

*A Free Verse Reflection on the Life of Jesus
(Inspired by Conversations with Donald Ohnegian,
Esq.)*

He started out young in the shop,
A tattered canopy held up
By rough-hewn poles and prayerful hope;
A bruising boy, hands like a man's,
Fingers thick, muscled for labor,
Arms, shoulders, back as strong as lives
Meant for hard work with wood and nails.
His skin, cracked and leathered, alone
Was proof against the mid-day heat,
And his coarse-cloth, hand-stitched garments
Sufficed to keep him warm at night.
We can imagine him content
On the whole with his hillside home's
Verdant, rather moderate climes.
By most measures not well-to-do,
His plying the family trade
Still provided him with income
Enough for an education
That insured his growth "in stature
And in favor with God and man,"
Till at last he could be about
What he called his "Father's business."

Strange saying! Even his parents
Had no idea what he meant.
Whatever he meant at the time—

It seems he meant scripture study,
God-talk with the best and brightest,
Nazareth to Jerusalem—
Eventually he grew up,
And set up shop as a rabbi,
Surrounding himself with students
Who, while not among the ablest
And most learned—babes he called them—
Somehow came to think they heard words
From him they could not live without,
Words of eternal life, one said,
Words alive yet today, some say.
So they followed, like Abraham
Of old, having no slightest clue
Where this one who said of himself,
"Before Abraham was, I am,"
Was headed. Back in Nazareth
One day, it seems he was headed
Off a cliff. The synagogue crowds
Which knew him from his youngest days—
"Is not this Joseph's son?" they said—
Took offense at what seemed to them
An impertinence: His reading
A popular messianic
Text as though, in their own hearing,
It was fulfilled. Had they heard him
Right, or had they misunderstood?
To our day the jury is out,
So to speak. But this much is sure:
No matter his favor with God,
His favor with man was fading.

At last it faded entirely.
His elder rabbis, some, not all,

Found him brash, even blasphemous.
With the mantle of a prophet,
And more than a prophet, he set
Himself to disturbing the peace,
Not the peace of Jerusalem
Only, but the *Pax Romana*
As well. Who was he to upset,
With one of his notorious
Cures, profitable trade in swine
Raised to feed the Roman army?
Who was he to say what should be
Rendered to Caesar and to God,
As if he were the arbiter
Of relations between the state
And religion? And who was he
To shut down the sacred temple
In Jerusalem one fine day,
Declaring it to be a "den
Of thieves," and no longer a fit
Place to worship God, "in spirit
And in truth," as if he himself
Could be "the way, the truth, the life"
Of worship for those who, with him,
As he put it, must be about
"His Father's business?" Who was he?

About this much there is no doubt:
He was a Jew, a religious
Jew, from his bruising-boy shop days
On through to what's called his passion.
He worshipped in the synagogue
And, till he closed it, the temple,
Though his reading of the Torah,
And the prophets, and wisdom texts

Nettled traditional scholars.
In other words, he set about
Reform with such authority
As set him apart. One followed
Him or relentlessly opposed
Him. With the Pharisees he shared
The doctrine of eternal life.
Yet he transgressed the boundaries
Separating Gentile and Jew
Clean and unclean, women and men,
Boundaries thought to be God-sent
To maintain ordered, public life.
Against the Sadducees, he taught
Torah's moral imperatives
With rigor. In fact he tightened
Expectations for compliance
With marriage and family law,
For instance, protecting women
From threat of capricious divorce,
And the elderly from neglect
By children held responsible
By God for the monetary,
Practical, and emotional
Care of parents in their decline.
Honoring father and mother,
Of course, was clearly nothing new.
Nevertheless, ways could be found
To keep the letter of the law
Yet break its heart. He'd have its heart
Restored. Was he, in fact, its heart?

His fate with imperial Rome
Was sealed when, at trial, he declined
To refute the allegation

That he was "the King of the Jews."
"You have said so," was his reply
When queried. That did not suffice
To spare him scourging, and a crown
Of thorns, and the rough-hewn, cross-beamed
Pole he somehow seemed bound to bear
And to be borne by from the start
Back there in the shop, a bruising
Boy, hands like a man's, fingers thick,
Arms, shoulders, back as strong as lives
Meant for hard work with wood and nails.
Could this, too, somehow be what he
Had in mind, but no one else grasped,
When, still young, he said that he must
Be about "his Father's business?"

12 November, 2010

COLD CALCULATION

(Ephesians 6:10–17)

The weight of winter's ice breaks limbs and bears
Upon the roof of heated homes the threat
Of sheer collapse. So too the crushing down
Of hate upon our generations—born
And reared for God-and-neighbor-love all free
Of fear's alloy, and not in any need
Of cruel preservation—brings to mind
How right must wield its might. Ice-threatened homes
Hold no pretense to luxury of peace
And quiet unprotected. Under threat
Of wintry hate felt bearing down, the call
To arms in preparation to defend
Familial affection's warmth and calm
Is swiftly heeded. This fierce, unsought strife
Is love's most dreaded deed; its coldest need.

19 January, 2011

AN AGONISTIC HYMN

*"They have treated the wound of
my people carelessly,
Saying, 'Peace, peace,'
When there is no peace"
(Jeremiah 6:14).*

*"O Lord . . . .
I have become a laughing stock
all day long
everyone mocks me.
For whenever I speak, I must
cry out
I must shout, 'Violence and
destruction'"
(Jeremiah 20:7–8)!*

I
Endlessly all around
Loud cries for peace abound,
A sure, full-throated bray
From those who see the day
Coming on when we're free
Of old divinity,
The myths of godly wrath
That place us on the path
Of sanctioned violence.
Is it not all nonsense?
One thinks of vast crusades—
In Europe once—cascades
Of cited, holy writ,
Threats of a brimstone pit

Or, on the other hand,
At last, a promised land,
A paradisal home,
The prayed for kingdom come.
Our brightest, best, as one
Say, "With all that we're done!
Old time faith's God is dead;
We'll trust ourselves instead,
And cause all wars to cease
By heeding calls for peace."

II

The thought has its appeal,
But then I turn and steal
A look within. The bleak
Prospect of which I speak,
Bloody and of soul-size,
Is mine alone. Most prize,
Most see within, a way,
Through innate strength, to stay
The course that makes for peace
Without a fight. They cease
To fear the wrath of God
Once thought to split the sod
Beneath our feet: earthquake—
Blood, fire—for heaven's sake,
Alarums from above
Rung in the name of love—
Fierce, implacable, set
At any cost to get
Back what belongs to it.
And yet, from where I sit,
This pacific labor
Most now seem to favor,
This peace apart from God

And fierce strife, has been trod
Down by the peccancy
Of a grim enemy,
An enemy within
Who, unopposed, will win
A savage victory
That spells the end for me:
All life, all peace, undone,
The reign of death begun.

III

First, and least important,
Disease, a mere portent
Of far worse foes to come
I'd be delivered from.
I'll go into that soon,
But first, affliction's tune:
A battle hymn! I'll take
Up advanced arms to make
War on insurgency.
So with some fervency,
I target killer cells
That, in increasing swells
Of violent attack
On innocent life, track
Waste and ruin all through
This aging body few
Give much hope of keeping
Sound for long. Still, weeping,
Retreating from the fight
Is not for me. The night
Gathers, but there's no need
To lend increasing speed
To its descent. Target
Terrorist cells! Don't let

Their deeds of perfidy
Win out over duty
Faithfully pursued still!
Cancerous cells I'll kill
With precision bombing,
Even though alarming
Collateral damage
Will be done. I'll manage
Radiation poison
Till my victory's won.

IV

Yet though I must enmesh
Myself in combat, flesh
Against flesh, my warfare
Deepens, and will not spare
Me soul-struggles of right
Against wrong, all the fright
Of evil against good,
What Luther understood
As Satan against God,
My soul a bloodied clod
On which the coming age
Does battle with, must rage
Against this time wherein,
Opposing God, my sin
Holds sway, and earns for me
The wrath of Love. You see
I'll not escape the stress
The present age no less
Knows: Peace apart from peace
With God finds no release
From bloodshed, all the blood
Spilt in the cause of good,
That is, in his cause, who

Was ever, only true
To our Father's will. Don't
Tell me Christ himself won't
Bleed for love. He has bled,
Once for all, in my stead,
In your stead too no doubt,
Wielding death, death, to rout.

V

You think not? Well, before
I said it: Most abhor
The thought of peace thus won
Through war, violence done,
God ordained, a tight vise
Of human sacrifice,
A jihad, age upon
Age, heaven sent, a Son
First, then followers soon
After. As writ: the moon
Turned to blood, and the sun
To darkness, till it's won,
The final victory,
The End for all to see
Of unholy terror,
Human sin and error.
"Peace! Peace!" You hear the call,
But there's no peace at all.
Wounds carelessly treated
Bleed still. And what's meted
Out for healing can't heal;
Therefore the commonweal
Suffers still. The brimstone
Pit widens. All alone
The prophet weeps, cries out:
"Violence!" But his shout

Is shouted down. Nations
Laugh. Congratulations
Go to the brightest, best,
Who, heeded by the rest,
Think old time faith's God dead.
They make their calls for peace
Sure that their wars will cease.

27 January, 2009

"May God deny you peace, but give you glory."

Miguel de Unamuno,
The Tragic Sense of Life, 330.

THE MOURNING AFTER EASTER

There is a leafless tree
That bore upon its limbs
The figure of a man
Heard breathing his last breath,
A sound of sheer silence.
And in that silent sound,
Disquieting good news:
Listen! *Crucifixus*
Etsiam pro nobis.
Is this the tree of life?

12 NOVEMBER, 2012

CREATIO EX NIHILO

"...behold, I create a new heaven and a new earth: and the former shall not be remembered, nor come to mind" (Isaiah 65:17, KJV).

The dust of generations lies interred,
Or floats within the gentle zephyr's swirl,
Or, boxed, lies in a columbarium
And waits—for nothing. Consciousness has fled
The precincts of the mind, and all the world
That sages sought to know has turned to dust,
To less than dust, to utter nothingness,
From which the world proceeded, so we're told
By scientists and theologians both,
Though some allege procession without cause,
While others claim, instead, the cause is God.
Pascal, who made his wager, bet on God,
Now tosses us the die and waits our call:
Shall what's been brought to nothing be restored,
Ex nihilo to nothingness again,
Or shall a living God make all things new?

22 FEBRUARY, 2011

SUPPLICATION

Now death comes on—and then, and then?
My soul finds rest as Calvin said?
My spirit seeks her home with God,
Till soul and spirit join again
At last, at last in bodied life,
The resurrection of the blest?
That is the hope scripture attests,
Abides, abides with faith and love.
O bless me now with faith, hope, love
That I may die—and live—in them!

5 APRIL, 2013

A QUESTION OF BEATITUDE

(Matthew 5:5)

After fire, wild flowers
Everywhere burning bright,
Delicate, slender, strong,
Grace the broad, ashen fields
With purple, pink, and blue,
Bring fragrance to the air,
Herald the cool, moist hope
That stirs beneath the waste,
The charred ruins of lives
Once towering, green, proud.
The conflagration passed,
Nature's vaunt set at naught,
Humbler forms of beauty
Inspire a sudden awe:
Shall the meek inherit
The earth, as has been said?
Are the mighty cast down,
And the lowly raised up
At last? And by what flame?

15 APRIL, 2009

Ordinary Time

◆ ◆ ◆

God Himself is the best Poet,
And the real is his song.[7]

E. B. Browning
19th Century

---

7. Elizabeth Barrett Browning, "The Dead Pan," 188.

LISTEN!

Through a deep wood,
Dark and windblown,
Distant traffic
Sounds as the sea
Sounds through grasses
Tall on the dunes.
Unintended,
An illusion,
A mimesis,
A virtual
Atlantic wrought
Of wood and wind
And distant traffic.

13 May, 2012

THE DUCK POND

(Ridgewood, New Jersey: Then and Now)

This scene is ours, as ever it's been ours,
Though peopled with so many thinking theirs
The quiet pond, the quacking ducks, the lawns,
Tree-shaded, where we'd kissed away long hours
In courtship of each other's hearts and lives,
While the roaring world round unleashed havoc
On romance, made lust of love, and courted
Violence, and gain, and wars unending,
Though this scene yet remains: the pond, the ducks,
The lawns, tree-shaded, and, if no longer
Hours to kiss away in quiet courtship
Of each other's hearts and lives, still moments
Such as this to share until our hours end.

10 April, 2012

TĚNEBRAE

A pillowed rest of deepest night descends
Now softly from the east, caressing dreams
Of you, my love, just as you are tonight
My dream, my pillowed rest, my soft caress.

9 April, 2012

TO THE CONTRARY

(Regarding the Holy Estate of Matrimony)

Marriage is not our right as now is said
But is a holy gift and task instead,
A covenant of grace sent from above
Enjoining us to live as one in love.[8]

10 April, 2013

---

[8] "Love comes from you, but marriage from above, from God. . . . It is not your love which sustains [your] marriage, but . . . [your] marriage that sustains your love." Bonhoeffer, *Letters and Papers from Prison*, 46.

INTERROGATION

How is it that so many whom we love,
Respect and care for, hold in high regard
Are cast down or cast down one another,
Are belittled, or each belittling each,
Are made a laughing stock before the world,
A world that cares not whom it makes sport of
So long as, raucous, it goes on its way
Inebriate with ridicule of all
Who, in long years gone by, were held in high
Esteem for daring life beyond their means,
With all their failures aspiration's wake
And not a sign of sheer hypocrisy
As is alleged by lesser souls now proud
In commentary on the passing scene?

1 APRIL, 2012

SPRING'S GLAD LABOR

The time had come—it always comes in spring—
To cut back the forsythia so tall,
So tangled, spread abroad, and so enmeshed
With all my lilies of the valley, white
And small and smothered quite enough with ferns
That I could barely make them show at all
Their tiny silent, gently bobbing bells,
Those harbingers of summer's coming on
With all its warmth and colors bright and gay,
So celebrating brimming life with joy.
Such signs of hope, it seems, require some work
If we would have them come to view at all.
To cut away the briefly golden vines
To see the evidence of everything
That is enduringly worthwhile,
Like warmth and color, beauty, gaiety,
Is labor glad as hope—and faith and love.

8 March, 2012

BARBED TRAILS OF THOUGHT

The wood was deep and thick with summer heat,
The path was tangled, bordered everywhere
With barbed wire brush so sharp one's clothing, pricked
Would tear clear through so that the flesh beneath
Might suffer ouch-sized wounds. I walked with care,
I watched, eyes wide, alert, each step I took,
And only briefly stopped to look ahead,
Or up or down or to my left or right.
But once upon a stop I stood appalled,
For there, just to my right, as I recall,
I saw a scene of silent torment move,
Just barely crawl, no destination fixed,
No direction sure, yet surely destined
To an end horrendous, evil, fright'ning,
Unjustified, unjustifiable.
A wounded rabbit bore its dreadful fate—
The burden of the swarming flies that fed
Upon its mortal wounds—no slightest grasp
Of its condition; and the flies themselves,
Of course, were innocent of thought. They ate,
As they were made to eat, the evidence
Of nature's seeming disregard of life:
The charm of cottontails frolicking free
Where human beings walk their tangled paths
In wariness of what can cause them pain,
However slight. That frolicking can lead
To mortal pain and anguish gives us pause.
That it can lead to torment stops us short
And sends our minds down barbed trails without end.

7 March, 2012

RABBIT FOOD

For the most part our lawn is rabbit food,
Much clover, weeds delectable and green,
And one lone rabbit nibbling through the scene
And making it a scene of nature's good
Provision for its lowliest, a rude,
A pleasant verdure granted to the mean
And humble creatures—rabbits, all—that glean
What's left them once our mowing's done. But viewed
From lofty heights where red-tailed hawks soar free,
Its rabbit food, alright, but not the lawn.
The nibbling rabbit is itself a meal
The hawk would glean from off this scene. I see
A wide-eyed prey by talons gripped and drawn
Tree ward toward hungry death, no slightest squeal.

8 February, 2012

PLANGENCY'S DRINKING SONG

For a Suicidal Soldier in Time of War

(May be sung to the tune Vesper Hymn, Attr. Dimitri S. Bortnianski, 1751–1825)

"Fragments of unfinished stories
Such as you'd have in your dreams,
That's what I've got for a life now,"
The besotted soldier screams.

Then he draws his knife and thrusts it,
An inebriate room swirls round
Stagg'ring souls make for the exit,
One drops lifeless to the ground.

Morning smashes through a window
Like a volley shot from hell.
"Get up!" shouts the too bright daylight,
"You're not dead yet, ain't life swell?"

Up 'n at 'em, dons his khakis,
Reels toward another day.
Nightmare over, duty beckons,
Soldiering, he makes his way.

28 December, 2011

TORTOISE MEN

(Matthew 8:20)

They carry their homes on their backs,
You've seen them, the tortoise men, stooped,
Yet confident of their cold right
To plod along the city's streets
Come winter's rain, or sleet, or snow,
Postmen, nothing to deliver
But themselves to darkened corners
To sleep off the effects of days
Spent talking to themselves aloud.
They seem to us more presences
Than persons, shadows of a life
We have been spared. Thank God for that!
Likely we'll never know their names,
And never talk to them except
To say, "Have a nice day," as we
Toss some dimes, quarters, or dollars
Into the needy cup or cap
They now and then extend our way.
Foxes have holes, birds of the air
Have nests, but these bent tortoise men,
Like one once called the Son of Man,
These have nowhere to lay their heads.

31 December, 2011

AN INSOMNIAC'S QUESTION

Of late my nights seem longer than my days,
Within, without, the night falls fast and deep,
And yet, for that, I've precious little sleep.
I shut my eyes, I dream, but no dream stays,
My dreams and I go on our sep'rate ways.
I'm conscious still of how my dark hours creep,
And yet I've scarcely any mind to keep
Them from their wanderings. My long night's maze
Of thought—all wearied—posts no exit sure,
Provides no hint of where I might find rest
From this accursed, long insomnolence.
Unrested, shall I miss dayspring's allure,
That wakefulness that cheers those *daily* blest?
Shall I forever lack their common sense
And from the dream of daily light demur?

8 September, 2011

THE TRIUMPH OF *TAMIUS STRIATUS*

(The Chipmunks' Mockery)

Darting, damnable, downsized, voracious pests
Have made for themselves homes all about the yard,
Multiple, non-foreclosable purchases,
Security, comfort in holes in the lawn
In myriad crevices in stone fences
Still standing from pre-Civil War farming days
When acres of strawberries had to be kept
Safe from lumbering oxen and angry bulls,
In the curved aluminum ends of downspouts,
Never mind scurrying evacuations,
Temporary, whenever storms send torrents
Rushing through from the Yankee Gutters above,
In safe nooks and crannies under the front porch
Where mothballs evict all the skunks and groundhogs,
But not these pert little rodent-thieves who eat
Freely from my garden and from my dear wife's
Bird-feeder. This is what galls me most of all:
That they eat to heart's content and then eat more,
Yet gain no weight, while I, at the thought of food
Pack on the pounds. It seems not even winter
Or the circling hawks above can thin their ranks.
So year after year, day in, day out I'm mocked,
I, the crown of creation, made sport of by
Darting, damnable, downsized, voracious pests.
Must Eden's curse, extend to this annoyance?
Must the *imago Dei* suffer such scorn?

10 SEPTEMBER, 2011

AN AGING, PORTLY POET-PREACHER'S CONFESSION

Though I'm not half the man I used to be,
It's clear to all there's too much left of me.

21 January, 2011

BRIEFLY STATED

(Conundrums of Postmodernity)

That there can be no metanarrative
Itself's a metatale that all must live.

We're told it's absolutely true
No absolutes can come to view.

With bated breath we wait to see
What's "post" to postmodernity.

Perhaps the "post" that's to be sought
Is unsaid sayings, thoughts unthought.

8 April, 2013

A TRIBUTE

To Dr. Evans E. Crawford and His Wife Elizabeth
(Ephesians 1:11–14)

Let me join my aging voice
To those voices young and strong
That rightly sing your praises,
Preacher, teacher, dean—and friend
Even to the unfriendly
And to the "poor in spirit,"
Poor in worldly goods as well:
A man in Christ visioning
A world where no one's forlorn,
Or hounded, or unwanted,[9]
And praying that world to be
Fervently, eloquently,
Your dear Elizabeth too,
With you and praying for you.
You are celebrated now
And will be celebrated
When all dreary, human hates
Are dead, laid to rest, and love's
Blest flame burns into the core
Of every last human soul
That gospel you preached, and prayed,
And lived, that, with you, we all
Might be to God's praise and glory.

17 JULY, 2010

9. These words were inspired by the poem, "Fredrick Douglass," by Robert Hayden. See Bontemps, *American Negro Poetry*, 119. This poem, "A Tribute," was composed, upon request, for inclusion in a celebration at Thurman Chapel, Howard University School of Divinity, honoring Dr. Crawford and his colleague, Dr. Gene Rice and their spouses for their fifty years of service to theological education benefiting the African American church as well as the church catholic.

I DREAMT A HUMAN SKULL

Last night I dreamt I saw a human skull
Addressing me as if with pow'rs of speech.
Through lipless jaws there came a soundless word,
A word not to alarm but comfort me,
And I was comforted and even warmed
By this unearthly specter strange, yet kind,
Whose eyeless sockets held a well-loved smile
That cradled me as with paternal care,
Assuring me, that even in a night
Of dreams macabre, I'd not be alone,
But tended to as when I was a child.
I almost called out, "Father!" though asleep,
I had myself no pow'rs of speech at all.
And then the skull was gone and seen no more.

10 OCTOBER, 2011

AFTER PRAYERS, A FACE

After breakfast, after our devotions,
Looking out the kitchen window, I saw,
And you believed me when I said I saw,
A man's face, sporting a full beard well kept,
Pleasant expression on his face, his eyes—
I can't remember the color of them—
Were looking in at me. His head of hair,
Red or auburn, thick, long, was neatly combed.
He seemed to smile a pleased smile, approving
What we'd been about just moments before,
Our devotions, our reading Baillie's prayers.
Oh, I'm sure it was not Baillie himself,
His ghost. You and I don't believe in ghosts.
I'm confident, in fact, that what I saw,
And, indeed, I did see it sharp and clear,
Was something wrought in fancy by my mind
And made visible. Imagination
After all, can play most peculiar tricks.
Nevertheless I was cheered that the face
I saw, really saw, was pleased to smile
And to affirm us in our morning prayers.

12 OCTOBER, 2011

TIME'S RECKONING

(John 8:58)

In the midst of time, Time itself stands still,
Eternity, that is, comes under siege
And history wreaks havoc upon faith
And hope and love which history cannot
Instance, prove, refute, praise, or claim, or laud.
Still tyranny of explanation storms
The mind. Humanity must cower now
Or flee into obscurity of myth.
True religion stands, stands and testifies
To Time, Eternity in human form
Prevailing over history at last,
And bringing to account before itself
Those endless skeins of thought, thought to be all.
History's true end: time eclipsed in Time.

16 FEBRUARY, 2011

AN EAST SIDE WISH

Alone I shuffle up the crowded walk
And hear, but do not listen to the talk,
The happy-hearted banter of the throng
That passing me strides jauntily along
This Sunday afternoon in early fall
Toward Central Park, its restaurants and all
Its fine attractions: frolic on the green,
Museum pieces waiting to be seen
By connoisseurs of ageless human art
Or nature's history traced to its start.
This moving converse, purposeful and glad,
Leaves me perplexed that I alone am sad
This autumn afternoon so bright, so gay,
And warm enough to make one wish back May.

28 October, 2009

IN ANTICIPATION OF DEMENTIA

(A Poet's Lament)

The willow's nearly bent in two by wind
And wintry rain, part ice, part sleet, part snow,
And the Japanese Dogwood's spindly limbs
Are twisted into spectral shapes that haunt
The lonely cabin with its door ajar
Battering the air like a one-winged bat
So silent in its struggle against death
One hardly knows its end is coming on.
By spring, surely, the cabin will be gone
As I, too, will be gone far, far away
From minding all I treasure: the willow,
The spindly dogwood, the ruined cabin,
Wind, rain, ice, sleet, snow, bats, and spectral shapes,
Imaginations conjuries that tease
What's left of memory with vacant scenes
That never were. I'll speak no more of them
To you, my love, for from you I'll be gone.

10 December, 2010

DELIRIUMS

The boy, terrified, twisting his hair, felt
What seemed a fire, fierce, raging in his brain,
One hundred seven degrees of fever
Flaming wild imaginings more frenzied,
More macabre than demon dreams, bedroom
Deliriums, a grotesque carousel
Of radiators grown up to ceiling height
Dancing, threatening to carry the boy
Around and away to some burning fate.
"Mommy! Mommy!" the boy cried, loud, louder,
"Mommy! Mommy! Come quick! Mommy!! Mommy!!"
Quickly as she could, ice-filled towel in hand,
His mommy came. She pressed the cold compress
Firmly against the boy's forehead. She crooned:
"Mommy's here. It'll be alright." The boy, soothed,
Slept at last. Never saw his mommy's tears.

18 May, 2011

THE GROCER'S LARGESS

(Circa 1943)

A Belated Tribute to Mr. Bernstein

We grew up less than well-to-do
Yet something more than outright poor.
Our bills were seldom paid in full,
Our fiscal situation dour;
But yet we'd plenty—it is true—
At each meal time, for Mom would pull
A miracle of tasty treats,
Like hashes made of ground up meats,
Potatoes, vegetables rich
In vitamins. We stayed well fed
Throughout our hard times—and the war—
Quite healthy, happy, that instead
Of angry, bitter to the core,
As some became who'd not a stitch
Of such help as had come our way,
Unmerited, I have to say.
The grocer drove his truck around,
Delivered packages galore
He knew that we could not afford.
"Oh, keep the change!" and what is more
He said, "You'll pay it afterward
When times are better." So assured,
They worked, my Dad, my Mother too,
Till we grew up more well-to-do.

5 November, 2012

ABREACTION

Young loves in boys like this boy were not told,
Were secrets kept so no one young or old
Knew how he felt. Sudden tears at a play
Or movie where romance was in display,
Romance full of that sudden happiness
Where unrequited love, requited, spelled
"The End," insured his throbbing loves were quelled
Sufficiently to help him keep his calm
And keep his feelings to himself. This balm
For adolescent drama served to bless
His untold loves with a dénouement sweet,
An ending satisfying and complete
At least awhile; till loves sprang up again
And filled his chest with secret, throbbing pain.

10 November, 2012

QUESTIONS OF FAMINE

(Amos 8:11–12)

Has the time come again, as of old,
The time of the terrible famine,
Not of bread or of thirst, but of hearing,
The time of wandering sea to sea,
Of running to and fro, North to East,
Seeking but not finding food for thought
Heaven sent, to soften hardened hearts,
Ears itching, alert, hearing intact,
But nothing to be heard worth hearing?

Has the heavenly host stopped singing,
(I am speaking allusively here,
In a figure), is the Voice beyond
The present human cacophony
Self-silenced for a time—or forever?

Or are they in the right who do not
Hunger or thirst because, as they say,
There is no Voice at all to be heard?

13 APRIL, 2013

AN ANTINOMIAN DAWN

*"If then the light in you is darkness,
how great is the darkness" (Mt. 6:22^b)!*

The sun declines from West to East
And darkness rules the day.
Thick Darkness stalks through waking hours
And night's light turns to gray.
For moonlight, moon dust all around,
The stars' light fades away.
And darkened sense now cannot see
Morality's decay.

12 April, 2013

ECCLESIASTES REDUX

*"Vanity of vanities, saith the Preacher,
Vanity of vanities; all is vanity" (Eccl. 1:2, KJV).*

*"…What profit hath he that hath labored for the
wind" (Eccl. 5:16, KJV).*

The abandoned pulpit echoes
(vanity of vanities)
A laboring for wind,
Some human suspiration
To give voice to a word,
A pacemaker of grace perhaps,
To strengthen the iambic
Of an old man's tired heart.

6 OCTOBER, 2012

FALSE ALARM

(Upon a Visit to the Cardiologist)

His auscultation caused me some alarm,
For why'd he pause right there and then if harm
He'd not detected in my old heart's beat,
Some weakness in the blood supply he'd treat
With interventions of some sort, a stent,
Or—God forbid!—such surgery as sent
Me once through doldrums of despair and pain
I'd come to hope I'd not go through again?

At last he pulled the stethoscope away.
He smiled. "I guess I'll live another day,"
I thought. He said the blood tests, too, were great.
On top of that I had a strong pulse rate.
Blood pressure fine considering my age.
Good news more than sufficient to assuage
My false alarm. Heart healthy, full of cheer,
He sent me home to rare, thick steak and beer.

29 December, 2013

WHAT IS THIS YEARNING?

(John 4:14[b])

What is this yearning gushing up in me,
This contradiction of the burning want
That threatens every moment to destroy
In conflagration all that I would keep,
Would treasure up—oh!—everlastingly:
The careless sound of children hard at play,
The knowing giggles of pubescent girls
Mature more than pubescent boys can guess—
Those knowing giggles innocent of harm—
The child at its mother's breast, nourished,
And warmed, and held in promise of a love
More lasting than all human loves can dream?
What is this yearning deeper than my thought
Of it, and deeper than my feeling it,
This ecstasy poignant as a song, more gay
Than colors splashed across an evening sky
Or bursting like a pointillist's bright dawn?

1 FEBRUARY, 2014

Poems Out of Season: Back Acre Remembrances

♦ ♦ ♦

Childhood is the small town everyone comes from.[10]

SAID OF GARRISON KEILLOR

---

10. The above quote is from an article by John Skow and Jack E. White, and titled "Lonesome Whistle Blowing," 68ff.

CONCORD GRAPES

Bordering the back acre—
To the east our vegetables,
To the west our neighbor's canna
All brilliant red and yellow—
Grape vines climb their trellises,
And, despite Japanese beetles,
Offer up their dark, sweet fruit.
Baby sister, big brother, and I
Pick the ripe grapes eagerly,
Eat some, and take in the rest
So that our mother can make
And jar the jelly we so love.
It's fun to break the paraffin
To gain access to the spread;
And the peanut buttered bread
Almost begs to be covered over.
We grant that wish, salivate,
And with mouths watering gladness,
Bite our treats with sheer delight.
Our mother seems pleased and proud.
Clearly these aren't the grapes of wrath,
Nor those of the little foxes
Who spoil, as the poets have said,
The vineyard of the family,
Turning sweet means to sour ends.
These are the grapes of concord,
Making of sibling rivalry
A taste-bud joy of ecstasy,
And granting to parental life
A moment free from sibling strife.

VICTORY GARDEN, 1943

We called it our victory garden
Though we dug, planted, weeded it
And picked the crop even while victory—
In Europe and the Pacific—
Was far from certain, and neighbors
Mourned their dead, rough plowed into foreign fields.

I was six, my brother eight,
My sister just four, but even she
Could help hoe, water, pluck the yield
In string beans, limas, peas, and sweet corn,
Tomatoes too. Beyond our garden
Seeded in happy-hearted hope,

Asparagus grew wild. My brother
And my father, with sharp, hooked blades
Cut the stalks well below ground level.
Why, I do not know, but my father
Insisted the asparagus
Should be cut off and gathered just that way.

Well below ground level, cut off,
Our soldiers in their trenches died
To keep alive hope of getting home,
Of ingathering normalcy:
Parents, children reaping riots
Of joy from their victory gardens,

And from wild fields beyond, fresh growth
From seeds buried everywhere—as lives.
Is there a resurrection of the dead?
Do we garden—dare we hope—for triumph?
Or is the harvest of our toil, parent,
Child, soldier, a Pyrrhic victory?

THE SHAMBLES COOP

There were no chickens cooped here.
The long, rectangular house,
Once their house, was made ours,
Was a shambles. Gaping
Holes in the roof and walls
Let in light and weather.
Floor boards entirely gone,
We walked two-by-four joists,
Young circus acrobats,
Remarkably untrained,
Flapping our arms like wings,
Trying to hold balance,
Failing, falling, catching
Floor joists in our armpits—
Ouch!—not wanting to land
In weeds and chicken wire.
Once I clasped a mud wasp
On my way down. My scream,
Heard for acres around,
Brought my mother running,
Her calm more salve
Than the thick adhesive
Ointment she pressed gently
On the red, raised, smarting wound.
Next day, forgetting
Injury to my flesh
And pride, I was again
On the beam, a circus
Clown of sorts now with my
Siblings. Ernie was twelve,
I was ten, and Patty
Eight. This was long ago.

Patty was the athlete.
Ernie was recovered
From rheumatic fever.
I was, time and again,
Recovered from my fears,
Almost. Some fears, it seems,
Last even after wounds
Have healed. Were poisonous
Snakes coiled among the weeds
And chicken wire? Once I
Thought so. Could've soiled my pants.
Are there up to this day
Perils lurking beneath
The floor joists of our homes,
Beneath the balance beams
Of prayer we walk upon
While roofs and walls leak light
And weather, and mother's
Calm lies quieted, cold
Among the wire and weeds
Of memory, circus stunts
Of nightmare or sweet dreams?
"Our chickens have come home
To roost." It's true enough.
The long, rectangular
World we've taken over,
Made a play-yard shambles,
Fills with wasps and screams.
Still, flapping our arms, and
Striving for balance, we
Make our way: acrobats,
Some of us, some of us
Clowns, all of us alive,
Chastened, and glad to be.

STRAWBERRY PATCH WORK CHRISTIANS

East of the victory garden,
South of the chicken coop,
The strawberry patch
Drew our summer attention.
Some of the berries we gathered
Actually made it
To the kitchen table.
The rest we picked,
Gulping ripe, red sweetness
By the mouthful.
We were not blamed for this
Unless we were supposed to be
Picking for the benefit
Of relatives or neighbors.
We knew too that mom and dad
Loved strawberries on their cereal.
So big-hearted as we were sweet-toothed,
And bent on doing unto others
As we'd be done to—
For we'd been told
To love our neighbors as ourselves
And to honor our father and mother—
We always saved some berries,
Some of the biggest in the patch in fact,
For them, for mom and dad,
For neighbors and for relatives,
Though our neighbors especially
Always had more
Of everything than we,
Our poor couple of acres
Surrounded by their blooming hundreds.

By 1947 they
Even had a television.
Besides all this
We told ourselves,
With some satisfaction,
That we were obeying commands,
Doing our chores,
Tending to our strawberry patch work.
And is not the laborer
Worthy of his hire?

BANISHED EDEN

By the time I could pick
From the pie apple trees,
As my mother called them,
Way to the back of our
Ramshackle back acre
Eden, the chicken coop
We played in had been razed,
The strawberries dug up,
The beetle infested
Concord grapevines burned out.
Asparagus still grew
Wild, but our garden spot,
A victory garden
No longer, was kept for
Pride, not necessity.
World War II was over,
Over some time ago.
My brother and sister
And I had our own friends,
So, though we worked a bit
Together in the yard
Or in the house, high-jinks
In our back acre grew
Less frequent. Often I'd
Wander the back acre
Alone, missing something
Yet looking for something
Too. Not another war,
That's for certain, although
One had been started up
In Korea, red hot
Furnace of the so-called

Cold War, East *versus* West,
Nuclear holocaust
The threat to end it all;
No victory in sight.
I settled on looking
For apples, ripe, no worms,
Not rotten, but meaty,
Nourishing to the core,
Neither sweet nor sour,
Pie apples for the pies
My mother liked to make
And which we children ate,
Eagerly, happily.
I especially liked
The crumb topped apple pie.
I picked carefully, but
The best apples often
Were found not on the tree
But on the ground beneath,
The happiest of falls,
Not like our human fall
Some call a fall upward
Into knowledge of good
And evil, and away
From Eden's naiveté.
I'm for Eden frankly,
For though I know the good,
I've slight strength to do it,
And though I know evil
Well, I can't avoid it.
I am missing something
As I pick or gather
Apples for mother's pie,
My childhood innocence
Perhaps: high-jinks without

Cunning, without a plot
Or plan for securing
Victory at the cost
Of sibling joy, friendship
With God and with neighbor,
Love, not calculation.
Perhaps I really
Never had what I now
Think lost, the innocence
Of Edenic childhood.
But then I know that fact—
If it truly is a fact—
Not as gain, but as loss
Not as a happy fall,
But as a fall from grace.
From my own back acre
Joys I am driven out,
I am exiled, banished.
It takes no cherubim
Or flaming, turning sword
To keep me forever
East of my back acre
Eden with its fallen
Pie apples and my fall
From grace, as I've called it.
Time has fled, I've grown up.
The apple trees are gone.
The back acre itself
Is gone, sold to make way
For houses and concrete
Sidewalks, macadam roads
And driveways, suburban
Growth to replace my own
Growing up, and learning
Something, missing something,

Yet looking for something
Too. Not another war,
That's for certain, although
I've seen so many, I've
Lost track. No victory
In sight. Humanity
It seems falls endlessly
Into knowing good and evil,
But with slight strength for good,
And great strength for evil.
Is there no tree of life
From which one day we may
Pluck victory as I
Plucked apples in my youth?
I am missing something,
Looking for something
Too, beyond the lost life
Of my banished Eden.

More Poems Out of Season: Labor Loved

◆ ◆ ◆

"Let the favor of the Lord our God
 be upon us,
and prosper for us the work of
 our hands—
O prosper the work of our
 hands" (Psalm 90:17)!

OUR FAMILY FARM

(Circa 1815 and since)

I

The land was theirs for the farming long before
The stone house, gone for good, was built to lodge
Our early (names lost) ancestors who kept
The barns and pastures, stables where the cows
And horses, oxen too, were housed secure
And cared for, working animals for all
Those farming needs: a family's milk supply,
The plowing, travel, carting to be done
To make strawberry growing hereabouts,
The best in all the east and well beyond.
So fresh and sumptuous the berries were
Mouths watered for them from nearby New York
To south and west to cities, villages
A country growing up had need to found.
The labor those young days was labor loved,
Was life and sustenance and commerce too,
A cultivating good for one and all.

II

No one remembers now precisely when
The house was built by hand that, standing still,
Inherited the hopes and memories
A family cherishes for holding on
When labor loved is threatened by hard times
And evils too long unattended to.
But 1839 is thought the date
The rambling, white, green shuttered house rose up.
Some decades then before the Civil War

Attended to the hateful clanking chains
Forced labor forged in brown, and black, and blood,
The house was there, and theirs a farming life
Of labor loved, as said before, free work.
It's not for us to know whether or not
They saw as scourge what brought the war or took
Some part in building soul train hideaways
To harbor runaways to Canada.
But New York state, just minutes to the north,
Was surety of hope dark passengers
Might make it all the way. And what was that
Beneath the shuttered farm house kitchen floor
(The kitchen add-on to the main house built
Only a year or two before the war),
That dry and rock-walled, trap-doored room of sorts?
What was it for? Some like to think for slaves
Bound to be free for labor loved, not forced,
Adoptive kin to farmers such as these.
A root cellar's more likely others say,
And farming logic holds we should agree,
Though what's in fact the case, who knows for sure?

III

Sometime before the 19th century
Was done, a schoolhouse built, new church set up,
A town cut out and named where the farm stood,
Our farming family greeted joyously
The railroad that arrived upon the scene
With promised easy access to supplies
And markets for their crop: those strawberries
So sumptuous, so sweet, so in demand.
Their labor, loved, met with prosperity,
Though only for a time. When war broke out
To "make the world safe for democracy,"
Though unsafe for enlisted warriors

Who now could not be hired to work the farm,
The labor once so loved turned into sweat
Of sheer necessity. The railroad prized
As boon soon turned to bust, for far out west
In acreage that stretched to miles, farm crops,
Including strawberries, were grown the whole
Year round. So family farming in these parts
Was hard-pressed to keep up. Sometime before
The 1940s, land was needed more
For housing than for farming. Soon the barns,
The pastures, animals so cared for once,
Were gone. The railroad, now commuter line,
Took former farmers to nearby New York
And to the world of banking and finance.
The farm was left to be sold off in bits,
A two lot bit inheritance for us:
A rock fenced acre-worth of memories,
A white, green-shuttered house, and there beneath
Our kitchen floor, a stone walled room sealed off
That we've no purpose for. Why it is there,
We'll never know. Our modest garden spot
Recalls for us lost years of labor loved.

THE HOUSE OF MEMORY

(Constructed Circa 1839)[11]

When the last shovelful of rocky soil
Fell upon the little girl's graves that held
The remains of childhood smiles he'd cherished,
And when the mother's love that brought those smiles
Later was covered over with the same
Heavy earth and the sweat of manly grief,
He headed down the graveyard hill toward home:
Stretches of stone wall set in place by hand,
Acres of strawberries planted for gain,
And the green shuttered farm house built to last,
Made weary now by weight of memory.

---

11. This poem is a reflection upon headstones found in Union Cemetery, Ramsey, New Jersey: James R. Goetschius, d. 1915, his wife, Eliza Banta Goetschius, d. 1913, and three of their children, daughters Margaret, Mary, and Rachel, d. 1864 from scarlet fever. The Goetschius farm dates back to 1815. The "House of Memory" was built by John P. Goeschius. My wife, Ruth Paula Goetschius Bartow (great, great granddaughter of John P. Goetschius) and I have the good fortune to live in the now one-hundred-and-seventy-five-year-old "House of Memory."

A GRUDGING RESPECT

You have to admire
The poison ivy,
The way that it shines,
The way that it climbs—
Refuses to die!

A LONG HOSPITALITY

Our one hundred years plus garage
Leans heavily to the right.
In storms it welcomes the rain.
Frightened chipmunks and squirrels
Find refuge in it from hawks.
Beneath its long-sagging roof,
Birds nest in safety and warmth,
Even the bats feel at home.
Often it shelters two cars.
Once it housed horse carriages.
Back then it stood tall and straight.
Now it leans heavily right.

A NURTURED HOPE

Our mowed green weed backyard,
Laced through with wild flowers—
Clover and violets—
Draws humming honey bees,
Lends fragrance to the air,
Gives promise untamed life
Elsewhere, gently infused
With unexpected care
And a vagrant sweetness,
May one glad day flourish
With beauty, charm, and grace.

A BRIGHTENED LABOR

The stonewall to the south
Of our antique farm house
Shows morning-glories gay
And honeysuckle vines,
"Virginia creepers" too
Metastasizing fast,
Reaching for the maples
Close behind the toolshed
Just ten feet to the north,
To drain the life from them
And pull them down at last.
We rip the "creepers" up,
Though they keep growing back.
This cancer surgery
Of ours is never done.
Still, we can take delight
That honeysuckle vines
And morning-glories gay
Brighten our long labor.
The maples, still alive,
Assure us in our hope
We'll keep malignancies
In check for years to come.

A BLOSSOMED SNOW STORM

A late spring snow of locust blossoms fell
In pink and white, so delicate, so soft
The grass itself seemed not to care a storm
Had hit and covered up its dark, rich green.
Oh, we were sure this storm was harbinger
Of fiercer storms to come. But for right now
This blossomed snow storm filled our hearts with joy.

FROZEN BEAUTY

(An Early Winter surprise)

Over and over again hereabouts
December's snows, if any, come on late
Then disappear as the mercury climbs
Leaving the year to end in rain and slush.
We've come to count on it: the melting white,
The black ice vanished from our walks and roads,
All early signs of winter washed away.
Yet now and then we get a cold surprise
Of snow on snow, of lasting ice on snow,
A scene of frozen beauty to be sure
Safely enjoyed from well without the scene
Inside a cozy, heated, windowed room.
Bold souls may venture forth into the cold
And so become part of the scene themselves.
But lovers of wintry art such as I
View it from a warmed aesthetic distance.[12]

15 December, 2013

---

12. "Beauty is the true form of distance." Hart, *The Beauty of the Infinite*, 18.

Concluding Essay

What "Is" Is—and Isn't:
The Fragile Indicative of Poetry and Preaching[13]

A POEM HAS A life of its own, comes about through an act of free labor, survives as verbal, vocal, and physical gesture, as ink turned into blood.[14] It is an "is," not a "must," or an "ought," or a "have to." It is indifferent to conscription, is incapable of being drafted into the service even of the poet's own life intentions, prerogatives, opinions.[15] So it is the natural enemy of propaganda, of words pressed into the service of the might that makes right. When Pilate said to Jesus, "What is truth?" (Jn. 18:38) he was not searching for an answer. He was dismissing the question. Tyranny has its answers ready to hand. The way it is and is to be has been determined by the might that makes right and that suffers no contradiction. Therefore tyranny and poetry are inimical to one another. They are in fact mortal enemies.

---

13. This postscript is adapted from an article I contributed to a *Festschrift* honoring the Rt. Rev. Dr. P. Surya Prakash (BA, BD, MTh, Dr. Theol.), Bishop-in-Karimnager, Church of South India. Previously published as "Poet and Preacher: Towards a Theo-poetic of the Spoken Word," in *Preaching in the 21st Century: Towards a New Homiletics*, edited by Vinod Victor and Amritha Bosi Perumalla (Delhi, India: Indian Society for Promoting Christian Knowledge, 2013) 4–20. Used with permission.

14. Bartow, *The Preaching Moment*, 15.

15. Guite, *Faith, Hope and Poetry*, 185–86, 192–93.

Jesus before Pilate, we may so construe it, was a *poesis* divinely wrought[16] in contradiction to the claims of Roman hegemony. The issue between Jesus and Pilate, therefore, was not somehow to find out the nature of truth through philosophical inquiry. The issue was to see whose truth would win the day. Those cowed by Rome had their answer as ready to hand as Pilate had his: "We have no king but the emperor" (Jn. 19:15). In other words, what is, *is*. The divine *poesis* that was Jesus therefore had to die to the powers of this world in order to survive as the utterly contrary indicative or "is" that it was—and is, and is to be. A poem, as I said, has a life of its own, and, following the life of the divine *poesis* we call "the incarnate Word," the life of the poem is cruciform.

But it is precisely that which was "crucified, dead, and buried" that "rose again from the dead" (the Apostles' Creed). Of course, as should be expected, the might that makes right forces, and those in league with them, claimed otherwise: "You must say, 'His disciples came by night and stole him away while we were asleep.' ... And this story is still told ... to this day" (Mt. 28:13–15). The latest version I've heard is that Jesus did not die, but only seemingly died. Once revived, he was carted off to Egypt to safety and obscurity. The inventive capacities of the propagandists for the forces of the might that makes right apparently are endless. Today they often claim the mantle of objective historicism that typically can brook no interference from anomaly. What "must have been" is what legitimately can be allowed as probable given the laws of cause and effect as operative in history as in physics. Yet the inventive capacities of divine *poesis*, if I may so put it, exceed all imagination. And even at the extremity of the Christ of faith vs. the Christ of history debate, they turn us toward the questions that trouble our answers, *all* our answers from whatever quarter.

Answers were at the ready even among those who all along thought Jesus to be the Christ, the Son of God. In the garden of his entombment he at first was mistaken for the gardener (Jn. 20:15^b). To others he seemed to be a stranger to Jerusalem and to the events that settled his own fate (24:13–18). Further, among others, he seemed an apparition, suddenly appearing in a locked room, stigmata and all, and speaking with disturbing poignancy: "Blessed are those who have not seen and yet have come to believe" (Jn. 20:29^b). For seeing is not believing, never was. Instead, believing is seeing. So the risen one appears yet today alive—and unnervingly present—as verbal, vocal, and physical gesture in the public reading and hearing of the

---

16. Ibid., 60.

Holy Scriptures and in that *poesis* of faith called preaching. He is *Christus Praesens*, resurrected presence, actively the subject (and not just the object of passing comment) in preaching.[17] For preaching, Christian tradition has insisted, is a spoken word, from a written word, attesting an incarnate Word ever and again "entering this life of ours to bear [itself] the weight of it."[18]

The incarnate Word, the divine *poesis* (as I have been calling it, following the thought of scholar/poet Malcomb Guite) is always *deus absconditus*, a presence of felt absence, a transcendence in fragile immanence, an incognito "is" confronting the thought-to-be-self-evidently-true and everlasting "isnesses" of exclusively human contrivance. Thus holy communion too, that proclamation of the gospel as a Visible Word (Augustine), attests a risen, truly present Christ with bread and wine taken and eaten in remembrance of him until he comes (1 Cor. 11:26). The resurrection then, as I shall dare to assert, is the divine *poesis* as perpetual interrogation. It is the everlasting question that troubles our answers on every front, a *poesis* appearing in the moments it is spoken. It is the final, fragile indicative that stands in utter contradiction to all thought to be—hoped to be—inviolate, eternal indicatives of human invention. Nothing merely human lasts. That is the "truth" Jesus taught, was, is, and is to be. It is no wonder then that the earliest witnesses to the resurrection "fled . . . for terror and amazement had seized them and they said nothing to anyone, for they were afraid" (Mk. 16:8).

From Genesis to Revelation, all biblical poetry (which is as much preaching as, for example, Milton apparently thought his poetry to be)[19] attests the contrary indicative that brings into question all thought to be inevitable, if not everlasting, human determinations of what is and ought to be. In fact, one reads on and on in holy writ yet comes upon hardly a word of it that is not poetry, or born of poetry, or yielding to poetry at last. "In the beginning God created the heaven and the earth" (Gen. 1:1, KJV). God did this, we read, with a spoken word, "And God said . . ." (Gen. 1:3, 6, 9, 11, 14, 20, 24, 26). The result is that we have a divine *poesis* of natural phenomena, wonders, and terrors to be pondered—and cared for (Gen. 1:28)—by the one (male and female) made in the image of God (Gen. 1:27).

---

17. Kay, *Christus Praesens*.

18. Wallis, *Worship Resources for the Christian Year*, 333.

19. Lares, *Milton and the Preaching Arts*. Note as well a contemporary pastoral homiletics text that treats of the preacher as a type of poet: Barnes, *The Pastor as Minor Poet*, 96–140. Also, Wilson, *Preaching as Poetry*.

CONCLUDING ESSAY

The scriptural witness to this *creatio ex nihilo*, this creation of all that is out of nothing,[20] plainly is itself poetry. But it is not mere surmise, or fantasy, or speculation. It is a reflective apprehension of a transcendent mystery that has taken hold of human imagination and caused it to "behold the beauty of the Lord" (Ps. 27:4).

> Ever since the creation of the world [God's]
> eternal power and divine nature, invisible
> though they are, have been understood and
> seen through the things [God] has made. (Rom. 1:20)

Scripture's poetry plainly is not poetry for its own sake, as if there actually ever could be such a thing. Instead it is poetry for faith's sake.[21] In that sense, at minimum, it is inspired—or else it is delusional. Faith in God as creator of all that is, ever was, or is yet to be, has been decried as delusional.[22] But it also has been defended as supremely rational, and, among human beings across millennia, seemingly inevitable.[23]

Pascal, we are told, not only grasped the immensity of cosmic material reality, but trembled before it.[24] For if beyond what is made (or perceived to be made), there is no Maker, humanity's insignificance looms larger than life, larger than death. All is entropy. The nihilists are proved right, and human existence, indeed all existence, counts for no more than the detritus that swirls around and around to the hole in the sink. We have in that bleak prospect reason enough to wager with Pascal on divine *poesis*, and for the God of Scripture, and not for the god projected out of human aspiration. The god conjured out of human nature's instincts and aspirations is no god. God the creator of nature and of human nature, on the other hand, the God whose *poesis* includes humanity made in God's image, can account

---

20. Peters, *God—The World's Future*, 128–31, 134–35, 149–313. Peters argues for the importance of *creatio ex nihilo* for biblical interpretation and systematic theology.

21. Bartow, *Dust and Prayers*, xi–xiii.

22. For Auguste Compte and his intellectual heirs, religious "mythology" apparently must yield to philosophical abstraction and thence to logical and scientific certainty. Compte, *The Positive Philosophy*, ch. 1. See Buttrick, *Sermons Preached in a University Church*, 204 and 222. Yet contemporary work in the philosophy of science and rationality seems to suggest directions of thought more compatible with religious insight and faith. Brown, *Rationality*, 137–228 and Van Huyssteen, *Theology and the Justification of Faith*, 133.

23. Guite, *Faith, Hope and Poetry*, 1–30.

24. This apprehension of Pascal is noted in Lewis, *The Business of Heaven*, 45.

for the fact that human beings do "seek him with their whole heart" (Ps. 119:2) and, so seeking, do in fact find him revealed in what he has made. Thus, when the great poem of Genesis speaks of the insignificance (or the coming to nothing) of human beings, it does so in a reflective apprehension of human beings "being returned" to the dust from which they were fashioned. No natural theology here, but only a theology of nature. God, it may be rightly thought, fashioned human beings for obedience to divine purposes in creation. Judgment, therefore, falls upon human vaunt and self-promotion (self-fashioning, if you will): "you are dust, and to dust you shall return" (Gen. 3:19^b). The theo-poetic apprehension of Scripture is that purpose is *given* to humanity by God. The return to dust thus implies a divine determination, despite all, to refashion humanity in obedience to God's purposes for it in creation. In a word, the return to dust is in order to the restoration of the *imago Dei*. In any case, all along, whether one thinks Scripture's poetic reflective apprehension of creation inspired or delusional, "it is strange dust that considers itself to be dust."[25]

It is strange dust too that discerns in its own nature, and not just in the great cosmos nearly beyond human reckoning, depths of danger and disquiet great as the immensities that troubled Pascal, and that—if we are anywhere near as honest and searching as he—trouble us as well. Poet Robert Frost spoke of these micro-cosmic threats. He spoke of a loneliness in nature that included him unawares, a succinct acknowledgement of the greater natural order's utter indifference to—incompetence to sense—the sensing creature that is humanity, sensing within itself a blankness, a benightedness.[26]

The holy, divinely inspired *poesis* that is Scripture, by millennia, predated Frost. And we surmise that it very well could have, indeed, must have, led Frost to see the mysterious, and, at times, disturbing depth of the made-in-the-image-of-God-one. The psalms are replete with praise of God for the God-created human being at spirit depth. From Psalm 8, praise:

> When I look at your heavens, the
>   work of your fingers,
> the moon and the stars that you
>   have established;
> What are human beings that you

---

25. Buttrick cited in Bartow, *Dust and Prayers*, xiv.
26. Frost, "Desert Places," 296.

> are mindful of them,
> mortals that you care for
> them? (Ps. 8:3–4)

On the other hand, from Psalm 51, we have a confessional lamentation that, while implicitly praising God, explores, in repentance, the depths of human disobedience and capacity for evil.

> Have mercy on me, O God,
> according to your steadfast love;
> according to your abundant mercy
> blot out my transgressions.
> Wash me thoroughly from my
> iniquity,
> and cleanse me from my sin.
>
> For I know my transgressions,
> and my sin is ever before me.
> Against you, you alone, have I
> sinned,
> and done what is evil in your
> sight,
> so that you are justified in your
> sentence
> and blameless when you pass
> judgment.
> Indeed, I was born guilty,
> a sinner when my mother
> conceived me (Ps. 51:1–5).

Then, in the New Testament, Saint Paul, not usually thought of as inclined to poetic utterance, ponders in prose-poetry his own sinful predicament. Clearly he sees his peculiar predicament as suggestive of the human situation before God more generally. He begins in lamentation, he ends (as do the Hebrew psalms more generally) in praise:

> ... I know that nothing good dwells within me,
> that is, in my flesh. I can will what is right,
> but I cannot do it. For I do not do the good

> I want, but the evil I do not want is what
> I do. Now if I do what I do not want,
> It is no longer I that do it, but sin that
> dwells within me.
> So I find it to be a law that when I want
> to do what is good, evil lies close at hand.
> ... Wretched man that I am!
> Who will rescue me from this body of death?
> Thanks be to God, through Jesus Christ our Lord. (Rom. 7:18–21; 24–25)

The poetic imagination in Holy Scripture, it needs to be said, is not only focused upon the apprehension of the speaking, self-disclosive God in the natural order and in oneself. It is focused just as surely upon human orders of common life and governance as already I have spoken of them. All of the Old Testament prophets were poets led to discern an always coming divine order for human well-being. This order, God's ordering of human corporate life, always is at odds with worldly hegemonic claims and claims of permanence for existing orders of governance no matter their popularity in certain quarters or the level of acceptance of the ideologies supporting them. Issues of obedience to God, therefore, have to do with the rectification of social ills and evils and not only with personal fears, puzzling, quandaries, and sins. No one has commented on this particular form of poetic consciousness, and its relevance to the task of preaching, more compellingly than Walter Brueggemann. Here I dare to sum up his position, and I hope this summing up is not a distortion or a facile reductionism. The prophetic imagination critically discerns, and holds in consciousness, a divine indicative, an instantiation of what is and is to be, that calls into question—and, indeed, finally is contrary to—all humanly created indicatives.

In the New Testament, poet-preacher Saint Paul gives word and embodied voice to this "counter indicative" of prophetic insight.

> God chose what is weak in the world to
> shame the strong. God chose what is low
> and despised in the world, things that are
> not, to reduce to nothing things that are,
> so that no one might boast in the
> presence of God. (1 Cor. 1:27–28)

In a striking literary *anamnesis*, Brueggemann joins our contemporary voices in a hymnic celebration crafted in deep awareness of the ongoing relevance of the poetic and prophetic imagination and consciousness of ancient times.

> . . . we sing ourselves free of Pharaoh,
> the Philistines and the Canaanites.[27]

Then Brueggemann goes on to remind us of the prophetic imaginative *poesis* that informs the doxology with which our praying of the Lord's Prayer concludes:

> We confess that it is to this God
> [and Father of our Lord Jesus Christ]
> that belongs "kingdom and power
> and glory," not to Pharaoh, not to
> Canaan, not to Rome, not to
> Babylon, not to the military
> industrial complex, not to the
> rulers of this age, not to the
> power of fear and hatred and hunger,
> but to the Lord who has said "fear not."[28]

"Fear not," said Jesus, "for it is your Father's good pleasure to give you the kingdom" (Lk. 12:32, KJV).

It is not infrequently observed that when tyrants come to power their first move is to rid themselves of poets, dramatists, novelists, playwrights, story-tellers, and perhaps also preachers. For the poet, the dramatist, the novelist and the storyteller, the playwright and the preacher (especially one who loves to tell the "old, old story" with ever new resonance)[29] cannot be, must not be, constrained by ideology. Preachers and poets cannot be, must not be forever in thrall to the given "is" or "ever must be" of tyrannically conjured indicatives, for then their work would not be art but advertisement, not *poesis* but propaganda. Isaiah spoke of a God whose "thoughts are not [our] thoughts, [and whose ways] are not [our] ways" (Is. 55:8). Saint Paul, echoing the prophets, turned their insight into doxology:

---

27. Brueggemann, *Finally Comes The Poet*, 71.
28. Ibid., 73.
29. Hankey, "I Love to Tell the Story," 325.

> O the depth of the riches and wisdom
> and knowledge of God!
> How unsearchable are his
> judgments, and how
> inscrutable his ways. (Rom. 11:33)

Perhaps the most poetic-prophetic affirmation of the ultimate fragility of all systems of common life and governance, of all humanly instanced and insisted upon indicatives, is provided in those texts that are clearly eschatological, and that promise great reversals in and beyond history. So for example, we read in Isaiah:

> On that day this song will be
> sung in the land of Judah:
> Trust in the Lord forever,
> for in the Lord God
> you have an everlasting rock.
> For he has brought low
> the inhabitants of the height;
> the lofty city he lays low.
> He lays it low to the ground,
> casts it to the dust.
> The foot tramples it,
> the feet of the poor,
> the steps of the needy. (Is. 26:1ª, 4–6)

Then, too, from Micah, this:

> In that day, says the Lord,
>   I will assemble the lame
> and gather those who have been
>   driven away,
> and those whom I have afflicted.
> The lame I will make the remnant,
>   and those who were cast off, a
>   strong nation;
> and the Lord will reign over them
>   in Mount Zion
> now and forevermore (Micah 4:6).

CONCLUDING ESSAY

In the history of the United States, a reversal, at least in some sense still in the making, is noted by Civil War historian, James M. McPherson, in his Pulitzer Prize winning volume, *Battle Cry of Freedom*. McPherson asks, "What would be the place of freed slaves and their descendants in the new order?" As a partial answer to his question, McPherson records this anecdote:

> In 1865 a black soldier who
> recognized his former master
> among a group of confederate
> prisoners he was guarding called
> out a greeting: "Hello, massa,
> bottom rail on top dis time!"[30]

The poetry of the psalms, like the poetry of the prophets, also reflects this divinely instanced reversal of the apparent "givens," the often believed to be inevitable indicatives of human socio-cultural life. In his magisterial volume on *The Psalms*, Samuel Terrien observed that the enthronement psalms of Israel have a thematic relationship to the deification of kings in the ancient Near East. Yet Israel's psalms also—and this is of crucial significance—possess an eschatological consciousness. In this consciousness, royal claims to (or attributions of) divine sonship (e.g., Pss. 2:7; 89:27), either in the sense of a metaphor of procreation or of adoption (e.g., Ps. 22:10–11), are pressed into the service of witness to "the messiah of the end time."[31]

In the New Testament, in Pauline thought, the messiah promised to Israel is attested not as a super-hero emperor but as the head of a body, *his* body, which is the church (e.g., 1 Cor. 12:12ff; Eph. 5:23; Col. 1:18ff). And, in making his point on this matter lastingly pertinent to human life in Christ (who is, let it be said, the proleptic instantiation of the restored *imago Dei*), Paul sings, and urges the Philippians—and therefore, by implication, those reading his letter yet today—to sing with him a musical poem inherited from the earliest days of the church:

> Let the same mind be in you that was in Christ Jesus,
> who, though he was in the form of God,
> did not regard equality with God

---

30. McPherson, *Battle Cry of Freedom*, 862.
31. Terrien, *The Psalms*, 51–52.

>   as something to be exploited,
> but emptied himself
>   taking the form of a slave,
>   being born in human likeness.
> And being found in human form,
>   he humbled himself
>   and became obedient to the
>   point of death—
>   even death on a cross.
> Therefore God also highly
>   exalted him
>   and gave him the name,
>   that is above every name,
> So that at the name of Jesus
>   every knee should bend,
>   in heaven and on earth and
>   under the earth,
> And every tongue should confess
>   that Jesus Christ is Lord,
>   to the glory of God the Father. (Phil. 2:5–11)

The prophetic, poetic imagination that apprehends in Jesus, in his cross, and in the lives self-subjugated to his rule and way—so bizarre by any worldly account of power, its acquisition and deployment—cannot be expected to be affirmed easily. Yet there are and have been, for over two millennia now, those who actually have taken Jesus at his word when he said:

> If any want to become my followers,
> let them deny themselves and take up
> their cross and follow me. For those
> who want to save their life will lose
> it, and those who lose their life for
> my sake will find it. (Mt. 16:25, also
> see Mk. 8:35; Lk. 9:29)

Likewise they have believed the testimony of the apostle Paul, who said:

> . . . you have died, and your life is hidden

> with Christ in God. When Christ who is your
> life is revealed, then you will be revealed
> with him in glory. (Col. 3:3–4)

Preachers with Christian poetic-prophetic-eschatological imagination over the years also have evoked in words and in embodied speech this same alternative cruciform indicative to the way things typically are thought to be. Helmut Thielicke, for instance, spoke of the triumphant power of God in Christ hidden in incarnation, but always about to be revealed at last in judgment decisive, irrevocable. In *Between God and Satan*, Thielicke wrote:

> So all the defenselessness of God's Son and his grace is a prophecy . . . for the open Lordship of God, which here has begun, and is only secretly present, while he waits at the back door of the world as a scorned Lazarus, because the rich lord in the house does not want him to pass his threshold. It has trickled already through the framework of the house; and a tremor as of abysmal powers shakes the pillars and facades again and again. But the rich man thinks that it is the stomping of his mighty foot that does this. And he lays costly carpet on the stone, so that the growling of the depths no longer disturbs him.[32]

A provisional summary: The theo-*poesis* of Holy Scripture, upon which the free labor of preaching is based, is manifest then as follows: 1) In creation narratives where an inspired, imaginative-reflective apprehension attests the cosmos' coming to be out of nothing *via* the spoken Word of God; 2) In the "fall" of the one created in God's image to "have dominion" (Gen. 1:26) over the natural order to that order's benefit, i.e., in accordance with the Creator's delight in his creation that is deemed to be good in its every aspect, indeed, "very good" (Gen. 1:31); 3) In the return of humankind to dust in preparation for the restoration of the divine image that, as we have seen, is proleptically instantiated in Christ Jesus; 4) In the prophetic/poetic consciousness within which an alternative indicative to humanly devised, authorized, promoted, defended, and enforced systems of common life and governance is imagined; 5) And in the gospel's announcement of an eschatological reversal of human vaunt in Christ Jesus crucified, risen, regnant.

---

32. Thielicke, *Between God and Satan*, 51–52.

This ultimate reversal of the human condition in Christ entails, too, humanity's glorification through its participation in Christ's death and resurrection. As already has been asserted, this that has been described is not poetry for its own sake, or poetry for the sake of emotional self-expression. Nor is this poetry as an indulgence of fancy. It is poetry for faith's sake. It is the exercise of a theo-poetic imagination upon nature, including human nature, as God-created. And it is the exercise of a theo-poetic imagination in the interpretation of the written word of the Bible as it bears witness to the incarnate Word that is Jesus Christ.

There can be no reflective apprehension of God's self-disclosure in creation, Holy Scripture, and incarnation if, at the outset, any possibility of divine self-disclosure is denied. Nature as a divine *poesis* demands a Poet. Holy Scripture as a narrative, poetic, reflective witness to God's self-disclosure in nature, in the history of Israel—in Israel's prophetic and wisdom literature—and, especially, in the incarnation of the eternally spoken Word in Christ Jesus, requires that a divine Word *is* spoken, is enacted. And it requires, in fact, that God himself is the speaker and the actor. The eventfulness of this self-disclosure of God elsewhere has been referred to by this present writer as *actio-divina*.[33] In other words, as Garrett Green has made clear, poetic imagination does not invent the transcendence it evokes.[34] To the contrary, it evokes a transcendence that impresses itself upon human imaginative and reflective capacity. Further, as Malcomb Guite brilliantly has observed and illustrated, even poets, who according to their philosophical scruples and presuppositions seriously question—or even rule out—transcendence, still are led to suggest the possibility of an apprehension of transcendence—and transcendence' apprehension of them—in their poetic efforts. In other words, in their own poems, at least on occasion, they bear witness to a possibility their unaided reason (divorced as it seems to be from their poetic apprehension) would deny.[35] So we are led to concur with George Steiner in what he argues in his much appreciated book, *Real Presences*. Steiner insists:

---

33. Bartow, *God's Human Speech*, 181.

34. For imagination's capacity to be addressed intelligibly by transcendence, esp. in relation to the Barth-Brunner debate regarding a "point of contact," see, Green, *Imagining God*, 28–29. For a refutation of a projectionist view of the relation of the imagination to transcendence, see, Green, "The Gender of God and the Theology of Metaphor," in Kimel, ed., in *Speaking the Christian God*, 44–63.

35. Guite, *Faith, Hope and Poetry*, 179–200.

> Any coherent understanding of what language is and
> how language performs ... is in the final analysis under-
> written by the assumption of God's presence ... the
> experience of aesthetic meaning in particular that of
> literature and the arts ... infers the necessary possibility
> of this "real presence" ... this study will contend that
> the wager on the meaning of meaning... when we come
> face to face with the text and the work of art or music ...
> is a wager on transcendence.[36]

One can believe that the God of Genesis addresses creation and, especially, speaks to the "crown of creation," i.e., the human being, because the author(s) of Genesis imagined God so doing, not on a whim, but on the basis of an experience of transcendence not conjured but confronted. One can believe that the prophets did not merely dream up a counter indicative to reigning paradigms of "the way it is and is to be," but actually were led to grasp something given to them. So they uttered their "Thus says the Lord" (Jer. 25:32 and verses in all the prophets too numerous for citation). Above all, when in the *Gospel According to John* we read the apostle's clearly theopoetical statement concerning Christ Jesus as the incarnate Word of God, we can believe it to be a scriptural *poesis* not only evoked but provoked by the enfleshed Word's confronting human consciousness with a transcendent reality not to be denied by those truly apprehending it.

> In the beginning was the Word, and
> the Word was with God, and the Word was
> God. He was in the beginning with God.
> All things were made through him, and
> without him not one thing came into being.
>
> * * * * *
>
> And the word became flesh and lived
> among us, and we have seen his glory, the
> glory of a father's only son, full of grace
> and truth. (Jn. 1:1–3, 14)

Even in their despair, the lamenting psalmists addressed the divine presence, though they addressed that presence as felt absence:

---

36. Steiner, *Real Presences*, 3–4.

> As a deer longs for flowing
>   streams,
> so my soul longs for you,
>   O God.
> My soul thirsts for God,
>   for the living God.
> When shall I come and behold
>   the face of God? (Ps. 42:1–22)

Likewise, nineteenth-century poet, Elizabeth Barrett Browning, used what is called "apostrophe," that is, speaking to a presence felt as absence, to seek respite from grief:

SUBSTITUTION

Elizabeth Barrett Browning
1806–1861

> When some beloved voice that was to you
> Both sound and sweetness, faileth suddenly,
> And silence, against which you dare not cry,
> Aches round you like a strong disease and new—
> What hope? what help ? what music will undo
> That silence to your sense? Not friendship's sigh,
> Not reason's subtle count; not melody
> Of viols, nor of pipes that Faunus blew;
> Not songs of poets, nor of nightingales
> Whose hearts leap upward through the cypress-trees
> To the clear moon; nor yet the spheric laws
> Self-chanted, nor the angels' sweet "All hails,"
> Met in the smile of God: nay, none of these.
> Speak THOU, availing Christ!—and fill this pause.[37]

Not least, an ancient theo-poetical construct from Holy Scripture, Psalm 23, spoken from memory in unison recital, provided hope—and a truly felt and truly needed transcendent comfort and assurance, in the midst of atrocity—right here and now in the early years of the twenty-first century. To demonstrate this, the following quotation is given. The quotation

---

37. Browning, "Substitution," 90.

offers comment upon a remarkable observation of Catherine Sasanov, a contemporary poet of considerable accomplishment. Sasanov states:

> There is something about poetry that is a vessel ready-made for holding our hearts. Psalm 23 is a poem, a song of trust, a belief that no matter how fearful the path, in life and death we will be remembered, loved, watched over for all time. In the multitude of interviews taped after 9/11, one man held it together pretty well while recalling the story of his escape from one of the two World Trade Center towers. He broke down completely, though, during his recollection of how people working their way down the stairwells began to spontaneously recite the twenty-third Psalm together. It wasn't lost on him—nor, would I think, was it lost on much of the TV audience—that this prayer of trust so associated with the dead had been recited by people who knew they were praying over what might end up being their own corpses.[38]

What we thus far have explored is a theo-poetic of the spoken Word that gives, it is hoped, some insight into the preacher's task in reading nature, human nature, the Old Testament Scriptures, and the apostolic witness to the incarnate Word in the Gospels and the Epistles (with special reference to the Pauline epistles) as an imaginative reflective apprehension of God's self-disclosure, that is, *actio-divina*. Preaching thus entails presence, alertness to God's embodied self-address to human beings in the person of Jesus Christ, and human beings' presence to and address to God and one another. In this matter, words count as verbal symbols implying vocal and physical gesture toward what must be faithfully (and not falsely) apprehended and explicated or reflected upon. Imagination and reason together and at once, therefore, must be inspired, Spirit-directed. In fact, as homiletician Luke A. Powery has written, preaching is *Spirit Speech*.[39] Preaching, therefore, must

38. Sasanov, "Psalm 23," 87.
39. Powery, *Spirit Speech*.

be prayerfully undertaken, and the words of the sermon must be carefully chosen. Perhaps here especially poets can be of some help, for they do care about words fitly chosen and fitly spoken, even when the words chosen and spoken contradict their own *a priori* understanding of what, to their way of thinking, it is possible to believe and to attest.[40] Words are fitly chosen when they have precise reference to things, thoughts, feelings, called forth by events, including *the* event of God's self-disclosure. Words are fitly spoken when they strike the ear and the heart and the mind of preachers and their listeners so as to elicit appropriate vocal and physical response, that is, embodiment and enactment of thought. Sermons call for response, and the response called for needs to be evidenced in the voice and body (and especially the face) of the preacher who, as was noted in my own earliest book on preaching, is a listener who speaks to facilitate other peoples listening.[41] A sermon that expects nothing from anybody (including the preacher) invariably gets exactly what it expects.

But we listen with our eyes, our posture, our sense of touch—and of our being touched—as well as with our ears. We listen with taste, with smell, with kinesthetic energy, with appreciation, with gratitude, with anxiety, even anger. We listen with an alert reason and with a quickened imagination. The witness of Holy Scripture to transcendence is of the earth. It is earthy, for God, as already has been noted, has "entered this life of ours to bear himself the weight of it."[42] The *poesis* of the sermon, Spirit inspired, thus is a *poesis* of bodily life, and of bodily death into life. Therefore, the creed: "I believe . . . in the resurrection of the body and the life everlasting" (the Apostles' Creed). All this has nothing to do with humanity's getting hold of God in order to get, among other things, the immortality it seeks. Instead, it has to do with God's getting hold of humanity and, in Christ, making it to be "to the praise of his glorious grace" (Eph. 1:6). The preacher, therefore, needs to speak as one gotten hold of, and not merely as one in possession of a few religious thoughts and a provocative comment or two on the passing scene. And what in this sense is true of the preacher is no less true of the poet. In framing of what I call fragile counter-indicatives to "the way it is," preaching and poetry are allied arts. Both are cries of earth and altar that can't be helped.

---

40. Guite, *Faith, Hope and Poetry*, 179–200.
41. Bartow, *The Preaching Moment*, 13–20.
42. Scherer, a prayer, in Wallis, *Worship Resources for the Christian Year*, 333.

Bibliography

Baillie, Donald M. *The Theology of the Sacraments*. New York: Scribner, 1957.
Barnes, M. Craig. *The Pastor as Minor Poet*. Grand Rapids: Eerdmans, 2009.
Bartow, Charles L. *Dust and Prayers: Poems*. Eugene, OR: Cascade, 2009.
———. *God's Human Speech: A Practical Theology of Proclamation*. Grand Rapids: Eerdmans, 1997.
Bartow, Charles L. "Poet and Preacher: Towards a Theo-poetic of the Spoken Word." In *Preaching in the 21st Century: Towards a New Homiletics*, edited by Vinod Victor and Amritha Bosi Perumalla, 4–20. Delhi, India: Indian Society for Promoting Christian Knowledge, 2013.
———. *The Preaching Moment: A Guide to Sermon Delivery*. Second edition. Dubuque: Kendall/Hunt, 1995.
Bonhoeffer, Dietrich. *Letters and Papers from Prison*. Edited by Eberhard Bethge. Translated by Reginald H. Fuller. New York: Macmillan, 1953.
Bontemps, Arna, ed. *American Negro Poetry*. New York: Hilland Wang, 1963.
Brown, Harold I. *Rationality*. London: Routledge, 1988.
Browning, Elizabeth Barrett. *The Complete Poetical Works of Elizabeth Barrett Browning*. Edited by Horace E. Scudder. New York: Houghton, Mifflin, 1900.
Browning, Robert. *The Complete Poetic and Dramatic Works of Robert Browning*. Edited by Horace E. Scudder. New York: Houghton Mifflin, 1895.
Brueggemann, Walter. *Finally Comes the Poet: Daring Speech for Proclamation*. Minneapolis: Fortress, 1989.
Buttrick, George Arthur. *Sermons Preached in a University Church*. Nashville: Abingdon, 1959.
Calvin, John. *Institutes of the Christian Religion 2*. Edited by John T. McNeill. Translated by Ford Lewis Battles. Philadelphia: Westminster, 1960.
Compte, Auguste. *The Positive Philosophy*. Translated by Harriet Martineau. New York: Calvin Blanchard, 1956.
deUnamuno, Miguel. *The Tragic Sense of Life*. London: Macmillan, 1921.
Green, Garrett. *Imagining God: Theology and the Religious Imagination*. San Francisco: Harper and Row, 1989.
Guite, Malcomb. *Faith, Hope and Poetry: Theology and the Poetic Imagination*. Burlington: Ashgate, 2010.
Hart, David Bentley. *The Beauty of the Infinite: The Aesthetics of Christian Truth*. Grand Rapids: Eerdmans, 2003.
Jones, David Hugh, ed. *The Hymnbook*. Philadelphia: John Ribble, 1955.

BIBLIOGRAPHY

Kay, James F. *Christus Praesens: A Reconsideration of Rudolph Bultmann's Christology.* Grand Rapids: Eerdmans, 1994.

Kimel, Alvin F., ed. *Speaking the Christian God: The Holy Trinity and the Challenge of Feminism.* Grand Rapids: Eerdmans, 1992.

Lares, Jameela. *Milton and the Preaching Arts.* Pittsburgh: Duquesne University Press, 2001.

Lathem, Edward Connery, ed. *The Poetry of Robert Frost.* New York: Holt, Rinehart and Winston, 1969.

Lewis, C. S. *The Business of Heaven.* Edited by Walter Hooper. New York: Harcourt Brace, 1984.

McPherson, James M. *Battle Cry of Freedom: The Civil War Era.* New York: Oxford University Press, 1988.

Powery, Luke A. *Spirit Speech: Lament and Celebration in Preaching.* Nashville: Abingdon, 2009.

Peters, Ted. *God—The World's Future: Systematic Theology for a Postmodern Era.* Minneapolis: Fortress, 1992.

Rolfe, W. J., ed. *The Poetic and Dramatic Works of Alfred Lord Tennyson.* New York: Houghton Mifflin, 1898.

Sasanov, Catherine. "Psalm 23." In *Poets on the Psalms,* edited by Lynn Domina, 79–89. San Antonio: Trinity University Press, 2008.

Skow, John, and Jack E. White. "Lonesome Whistle Blowing." *Time* 126:18 (Nov. 4, 1985) 68ff.

Steiner, George. *Language and Silence: Essays on Language, Literature, and the Inhuman.* New Haven: Yale University Press, 1998.

———. *Real Presences.* London: Faber and Faber, 1989.

Tennyson, Alfred Lord. Edited by Horace E. Scudder. *The Poetical Works of Alfred Lord Tennyson.* New York: Houghton Mifflin, 1898.

Terrien, Samuel. *The Psalms: Strophic Structure and Theological Commentary.* Grand Rapids: Eerdmans, 2003.

Thielicke, Helmut. *Between God and Satan.* Translated by C. C. Barber. Grand Rapids: Eerdmans, 1958.

Van Huysteen, Wentzel. *Theology and the Justification of Faith: Constructing Theories in Systematic Theology.* Grand Rapids: Eerdmans, 1981.

Wallis, Charles L., ed. *Worship Resources for the Christian Year.* New York: Harper, 1954.

Walsh, Chad. *Garlands for Christmas.* New York: Macmillan, 1965.

Wilson, Paul Scott. *Preaching As Poetry.* Nashville: Abingdon, 2014.

www.ingramcontent.com/pod-product-compliance
Lightning Source LLC
Chambersburg PA
CBHW032231080426
42735CB00008B/803